Introduction To The Vitaliy Balin Complete 5 Book Collection

This book is a collection of all five of my books. Four of my books are related to political science, while the fifth is a science fiction book. The first book is Vitaliy's Viewpoint On History, which details World War II and the history of the Israeli-Palestinian Conflict. The second book is My Moderately Centrist Viewpoint, which is about the need for a third moderately centrist political party in the United States. The third book is Kuwait, Qatar, And Israel, which is about my time as a Soldier in the U.S. Army, as well as my time in Kuwait, Qatar, and Israel, and how those events shaped my views for Middle East peace. The fourth book is Jerusalem 2100 AD, which starts out from the Middle East Peace Process in 2018 AD all the way through to humans exploring space in 2100 AD and beyond. The fifth book is Spaceship Palestine, Spacecraft Israel, which is about a future where those who want to rule Earth and their alien allies want to keep humans from exploring space.

Vitaliy's Viewpoint On World War II History, Israel And Palestine

In 1914-1918, during World War I, the British promised the Arab People their own sovereignty if they helped them defeat the Ottoman Empire. Several negotiations followed and eventually after the Ottoman Empire and Germany were defeated by the Allied Powers in World War I, the British Mandate came about. The

French and the British began to carve up the Middle East region, formerly governed by the Ottoman Empire into countries. Palestine and Jordan became part of the British Mandate. The Arab people who lived in Palestine wanted a State that they could call their own. The Jewish people, many of whom lived in Europe during a rise in anti-Semitism, wanted a state to call their own too, also in Palestine.

In the 1920's and 1930's, after Adolf Hitler came to power in Nazi Germany, many Jews in Europe wanted to escape Europe and either come to America or come to Palestine. Several ships which carried Jewish refugees in the late 1930's from Europe to America were turned away from America's shores. One of those ships was the St. Louis. It carried about 1,000 refugees or so and was turned away. Many Jews came to Palestine, which the British initially allowed. But by the late 1930's and early 1940's, the British not only disallowed more Jewish immigration to Palestine, because of mass Arab protests, but turned over the matter to the United Nations.

In 1939, Hitler invaded Poland. This started World War II. Before that, in 1933, Hitler had Nazi Germany pass the Nuremberg Laws. These laws took away rights from Jews and other minorities. The Jewish People who lived in Germany and Europe at the time knew it was time to leave. Palestine, by the 1930's and 1940's had both a sizeable Jewish and sizeable Arab population. Nationalistic sentiments between Jewish settlers in Palestine and the Arab population lead to a boiling point at times.

In 1941, Nazi Germany broke a non-aggression pact with Joseph Stalin and invaded Russia. In the same year, Japan attacked Pearl Harbor in Hawaii on December 7th, 1941. By 1942, victories in the Pacific such as the Battle of Midway had turned the tide of the war in favor of America. In the Battle of the Atlantic, Nazi Germany fought American naval surface ship and submarine forces with their own naval surface ship and submarine forces. Also, by 1942 and 1943, the U.S. was bombing Germany's military sites from the air from bases in Great Britain.

From 1942 through 1943, the Soviet Union fought a battle in Stalingrad, Russia against Nazi Germany. After suffering many casualties, the Soviet Union eventually turned the tide against Nazi Germany and defeated the Nazis in a major blow against the Nazi regime. During the same time, Great Britain and the United States flanked Nazi tank forces in North Africa and defeated them. The man who defeated Nazi General Erwin Rommel (known as the Desert Fox) was American General George S. Patton. This campaign successfully cut off Nazi Germany's oil supply to their main forces in mainland Europe. At the same time, another contingent of U.S. forces invaded Sicily and then mainland Italy to stop Nazi and Nazi-allied forces from continuing to occupy Italy. Italy was eventually liberated and Italian resistance forces captured and killed Benito Mussolini, who was the dictator of Italy at the time.

Also during the 1940's, Norwegian and French resistance forces, the French resistance forces being called the Maquis, successfully destroyed heavy water reactor facilities throughout Europe, most notably in Norway. Also, American and British airstrikes carried out from British territory successfully aided in the destruction of these heavy water reactors. Both sabotage by the Maquis and other resistance forces and airstrikes on German military targets that were working on heavy water reactors were necessary to prevent Germany from developing the world's first atomic bomb.

On June 6, 1944, the Allies, led by Great Britain and the United States, invaded Normandy in France. After a heavy day of fighting, the British and the United States forces took control of the beach by the end of the day with thousands of casualties. After several months, the United States managed to fight its way to the border with Germany. After fighting the Battle of the Bulge and several other battles, the U.S. made its way into mainland Germany. Russia also pushed the Germans back from its Soviet territory all the way back into Germany. On the Pacific Front, the United States Marines and United States Navy went from island to island, fighting the Japanese. Eventually the Japanese were nearing defeat.

In April of 1945, sensing an impending defeat, Adolf Hitler and his trusted Lieutenants locked themselves up in his underground bunker. They then took cyanide capsules, thereby killing themselves. Hitler took a cyanide capsule and then shot himself with his personal sidearm. Hitler was now dead and the war was coming to an end. In August 6th of 1945, the United States bombed Hiroshima with an atomic bomb called Little Boy from a plane called the Enola Gay. On August 9th of 1945, the United States bombed Nagasaki with another atomic bomb. Both of these cities were in Japan and both of them suffered severe casualties, with over 100,000 initial casualties reported from the blast wave of the atomic bomb on both August 6th and August 9th. Hitler's top Generals surrendered to the Soviet Union, Great Britain, France, and the United States in May of 1945. This ended the European theater of World War II. In September of 1945, the Japanese forces surrendered to the United States. This ended World War II.

In 1945, towards the end of World War II, the Soviet Union liberated many Polish death camps and prisoner of war camps where many Soviets, Jews, Gypsies, Homosexuals, and other persecuted minorities were being held. The Americans in Germany saw the labor and death camps and saw many emaciated starved Jews working there. A wave of regret and sympathy hit the United States, the Soviet Union, and the whole world with what they saw. Many people wished that they could do more.

In 1947, the newly founded United Nations decided to create a Jewish state in Palestine to compensate the Jewish people for their suffering in World War II. The Palestinian peninsula would be split roughly in half, with the Jewish State getting half of the land and the Arab State getting the other half of the land. In May of 1948, Israel, agreeing with the United Nations resolution, declared its independence. All of the Arab States objected to this resolution and declared war on the newly founded State Of Israel. Many Arab countries invaded Israel and Israel fought back with rifles, Jewish volunteers from around the world, and several tanks and several aircraft that Israel procured over time. Israel fought long and hard and the Arab States retreated. By 1949, Israel gained more territory all the way through West Jerusalem. It did not have the West Bank and Gaza strip and Golan Heights yet though.

In 1956, Israel invaded the Sinai Peninsula and started moving in the direction of the Suez Canal after Egypt nationalized the Suez Canal and after Egypt blocked the Straits of Tiran to Israeli shipping. Great Britain and France also invaded the Sinai Peninsula. The United States and The Soviet Union, not wanting this crisis to lead to a greater Middle East War, went to the United Nations and basically sued for peace.

In 1967, Egypt blockaded the Straits of Tiran once again to Israeli shipping. Egypt, Jordan, and Syria massed their armies along Israel's borders. In June of 1967, Israel attacked first and decimated Egypt's Air Force, which was mostly on the ground with the pilots away from the planes. Israel defeated the combined forces of Egypt, Jordan, and Syria in six days and acquired the entire Sinai Peninsula and Gaza Strip from Egypt, the West Bank and East Jerusalem from Jordan, and the Golan Heights from Syria.

In 1973, the Yom Kippur War happened. Yom Kippur in Hebrew means Day of Atonement. Israel was hit with a surprise attack by Egypt and Syria while many members of the Israeli military were praying. Israel suffered heavy casualties but eventually beat back Egypt and Syria. During the war, Israel did lose part of the Suez Canal zone and a small part of the Sinai back to Egypt.

This led to Israel wanting to negotiate with Egypt for peace.

In 1979, Israel and Egypt formalized a peace treaty and Israel withdrew from the Sinai Peninsula. This led to everlasting peace between Egypt and Israel. In 1982, Israel invaded Lebanon to stop Palestinian Liberation Organization (PLO) attacks that came from Lebanon into Israeli territory. Israel stayed in Lebanon until 2000, when it withdrew from Southern Lebanon. In 2005, Israel withdrew from Gaza. In 1990-1991, Iraq's Saddam Hussein fired scud missiles into Israel and the United States asked Israel to stay out of the Gulf War because the United States did not want to lose the Arab coalition that backed the United States after Hussein invaded Kuwait.

In 2006, Israel fought the 2nd Lebanon War against Hezbollah (The Party of God, in Arabic). Israel fought this war as a response to two of its Israel Defense Force Soldiers being captured by Hezbollah. At the end of the war, Israel eventually withdrew from Lebanon again. In 2008-2009, Israel fought a war in Gaza to stop rocket fire from coming into Israel.

Fast forwarding to the present, in 2018, I feel that Israel and the Palestinians need a Two-State Solution. If the United States can defeat Nazi Germany, if the United States can put a man on the moon in 1969, and if the United States can fight for freedom and equality worldwide, then I know that the United States can achieve peace for the Israelis and Palestinians. I agree with Israel's centrist Kadima Party's approach. Kadima means 'forward' in Hebrew. Israel should withdraw militarily from the West Bank and support the creation of a Palestinian State in the West Bank and Gaza. Based on the history of the conflict, I feel that a Palestinian State is necessary so both Peoples, the Jewish People and the Palestinian People, survive into the future as a People.

An Introduction To My Moderately Centrist Viewpoint

First and foremost, before we get into political parties, I have to say that I am an American first. Then I am a U.S. Army Veteran second. Then I am the political group that I belong to. But having said this, I feel that the Two-Party system in America is not working as well as it should. I feel that we need a third party. We need a new political party in Congress between the Democrats and the Republicans. We need a more moderate and more centrist party. We need something that I will call a moderately centrist party.

Chapter 1: Liberal, Then Conservative, Liberal, Then Conservative

Throughout most of my life, my political opinions vacillated. In Middle School, the economy was great under President Bill Clinton, and we were at peace (peacetime) and this made me feel great about Mr. Clinton. I considered myself a liberal. In High School, President George W. Bush brought our country into the War on Terror and I supported him because he was protecting our country from any further harm, like the Al Qaeda attacks that occurred on 9/11/2001. Mr. Bush's policies and his quick response to stopping Al Qaeda made me an instant conservative. So from 2001 through 2003 I was a conservative.

In 2004, Mr. John Kerry ran for President of the United States. I supported him as he is a veteran of the Vietnam War and I have a great deal of respect for veterans. So I became a liberal again. Then in 2008, Mr. John McCain ran for President and like with Mr. Kerry, he is also a veteran of the Vietnam War. And so I became a conservative.

My political opinions were wavering. I kept switching political viewpoints. One minute I was supporting Democrats and the next minute I was supporting Republicans. However, my viewpoints are fairly unique for any one major political group, but not unique to many Americans in the center of the political spectrum. Many Americans differ on many issues and do not side fully with one platform or another. The same is true for me.

You see, I am pro-Second Amendment, but anti-death penalty. I am for religion, but respect atheists. I support Capitalism, but know that in two hundred or three hundred years, we will need to get rid of it. So I am neither too far to the right nor too far to the left. I am what you would call a moderate conservative. That is what I call myself, but I feel, deep down, that I have more in common with centrist liberals than I do with right-wing conservatives.

Let me explain. I support gun rights because at one point, Joseph Stalin, the leader of The Soviet Union, said that he would never invade the United States because every American has a gun. This is why we need the 2nd Amendment. It is important for national security in case of a foreign invasion. I am anti-death penalty, although I am a moderate conservative, because I know that once in a while, an innocent person is either executed or unjustly sits on death row for decades at a time. Don't get me wrong, I do support life in prison without the chance of parole for the most heinous of crimes, but I do not support the death penalty.

I support religion. I spent a good chunk of my free time during my university days studying the Abrahamic faiths of Judaism, Christianity, and Islam. I love the idea of Abraham being the father to all mankind and of Moses parting the Red Sea. I love the idea that through faith in Jesus a Christian can be forgiven for their sins. I love the idea of the Prophet Muhammad being a Messenger of God, along with the other prophets of Judaism and Christianity, whom are also the Prophets of Islam. I feel that we need to study religion as it teaches us about the origins of many of our first and even last names, and it teaches us how we progressed as a society. But I do respect atheists. I myself will not identify as a theist or atheist, but will say that I am secular. I feel that atheists have the right to not believe in God because they do make good points in that they feel that what religion explains today science may explain tomorrow. I have always thought that since God is omnipotent, nothing humans can say about Him can hurt Him. Whether or not they believe in Him cannot hurt him as well. That is why I firmly believe that the religious person and the atheist deserve equal respect.

When it comes to capitalism, we need it right now because we have limited resources and limited money. We cannot provide for everyone in the world, and so we have many countries with many different types of currency sharing differing amounts of natural resources, based on population usually. Not always, sometimes richer countries get more natural resources, but it is generally based on population. That is how we distribute funds and resources, through countries. But in three hundred to five hundred years from now, when we eliminate poverty and have unlimited energy resources through advances of technology, we will be able to eliminate the need for smaller countries and for capitalism and have a type of socialism in place and a one world government. But for now, this system works best and that is why the U.S. and other countries that have capitalism should keep it in place. As you can see, even my views on economics are more balanced and not specifically left or right, but in the center.

Chapter 2: I Am Inspired By Israel's Kadima Party

In 2005, Israel was basically frustrated with a lack of a Two-State Solution to the Israeli-Palestinian Peace Process. So Israeli Knesset (Israeli Parliament) members like Ehud Olmert and Tzipi Livni formed the Kadima Party, with the word Kadima meaning 'forward' in Hebrew. Kadima is a centrist party that does not favor a full One State Solution like some Israeli liberal Labour Party members do, nor does it favor expanding Israeli settlements in the West Bank, like many conservative Israeli Likud Party members do. It supports a middle-ground Two-State Solution, as do I.

In life, there were many times that I made compromises. And in politics, people have to make compromises. So why can't we have a centrist political party? I feel that we can use Senator Joseph Lieberman as an example. He used to be a Democrat, but when Senator John McCain (a Republican) ran for President, Senator Lieberman supported his views, and became an Independent that usually voted with Republicans. I feel that all the Independents in the U.S. House and U.S. Senate, both chambers of Congress, should form a third moderately centrist party.

I do not yet know what the moderately centrist position will be, or what the party will be called, but I know it will be a middle ground between the liberal party the Democrats and the conservative party the Republicans.

Chapter 3: A Three Party System Will Work

If we have a three party system, then like the chapter title suggests it will work. If there is a gridlock in Congress, and there is a bill that most of the American public wants to see passed (many of whom are moderate conservative Republicans and centrist liberal Democrats), then a group of conservative Democrats, Liberal Republicans, and members of the newly founded moderately centrist party will vote as a bloc together and get the issue most of the American people want to pass passed.

You are probably wondering by now why I call it the moderately centrist party. Well, because you see how many Americans are either slightly liberal or slightly conservative. No one is one thing or another perfectly, but all of us go to one side of the political spectrum or another for an idea, and then the other side of the political spectrum for another idea, therefore we can be liberal on some things and conservative on others. And for most people, it balances out to being moderately centrist. Why only moderately centrist and not just centrist? This is because we tend to favor one political party's platform or another's more. This is fine, I feel. I will discuss this in the next chapter.

Chapter 4: Democrats And Republicans

Democrats believe in more social program spending while Republicans believe in pulling oneself up by the bootstraps. Democrats tend to be more secular while Republicans tend to be more religious. Democrats tend to support the 2nd Amendment as a collective right and Republicans tend to support it as an individual right. Democrats tend to be more anti-war while Republicans believe more in interventionism to spread democracy and other American ideals. I can go on and on about the differences.

I tend to lean Republican. But like I said earlier in this book, I have some liberal democratic positions along with some conservative republican positions. I feel that since Republicans tend to increase military spending, this makes me believe that Republicans care about our military a lot. And this is important to me as a Veteran. That is why I tend to support the Republican Party.

We can all follow one party or another, but if most of us are moderate, as most Americans seem to be, we need to find a moderately centrist party that can bridge our divide.

Chapter 5: Mr. Trump Is Elected To Office

From what I hear, up until 2008, the President of The United States, Mr. Donald J. Trump, was a Democrat. Now, as I am writing this in 2018, he is a Republican. So I am not the only one that switches political party allegiance.

He has the number one moderate position. He supports increasing military spending but he does not support going to war unless absolutely necessary. This is the perfect example of a moderate centrist. I do not really consider him a Republican, but someone who does the right thing to help the American People out. He does the right thing to make the world and our lives better.

Another thing I like about Mr. Trump is his honesty. He was elected on the platform that he will help the

American people, save American jobs, and boost our economy. He did just that in a year and half and this usually takes most Presidents four to eight years to accomplish the same thing.

Like I said earlier in the chapter, while Mr. Trump identifies as a Republican, him both switching parties and him supporting the military but avoiding war except as an absolute last resort, makes him moderately centrist.

Chapter 6: I Would Register With A Moderately Centrist Party If…

I would register with a moderately centrist party if it was a big party in the halls of Congress. I do not want to register with small parties because many of them have too many differing viewpoints and do not get their issues on the ballot. A large moderately centrist party (combining both formerly conservative Democrats and formerly liberal Republicans) with one central viewpoint that combines the best of the Democrats and the best of the Republicans is what would get me to vote for and register as a member of that party.

The United States of America, like the former President of the United States, Mr. Barack Obama once said, is exceptional. Although the President of the Russian Federation, Mr. Vladimir Putin, took exception to this and went on Russian media to state that no one is exceptional, I disagree with Mr. Putin and others who think like him. I feel that America is indeed exceptional. That is why I feel that Congress needs to reflect this exceptionalism. Don't get me wrong. The Republicans and Democrats in Congress are doing a great job. But we need an even more diverse set of viewpoints. That is why a third party is needed. Someone in the middle can bridge the gap between two opposing viewpoints. And even if the voice in the middle is not the one that either speaks the loudest or gets its voice heard, it will still mean that there will be three opinions in both Chambers of Congress, the House and Senate, and not only two opinions.

Chapter 7: Three Opinions Instead Of Two

A larger diversity of opinion in the Halls of Congress will allow for even more innovation in our country. Three voices instead of two and three opinions instead of two will allow for the leadership of our country to see 33% more information or at least interpret information 33% differently. If 1/3 or up to 1/3 of

Congress is part of a moderately centrist party, then we will have change for the better in this country.

We will be able to pass laws not just from the left and right, but from the center too. And the diversity of opinion will work even if we only have a small handful of moderately centrist individuals in Congress. As long as the party is in Congress, and as long as tens of millions of Americans register for that party, a third voice is sure to be heard.

This worked well in Israel. I don't believe that Israel built the first commercially mass produced cell phone in the world in the 1990's by not having a diversity of opinion. Like I said in an earlier chapter, this diversity of opinions is also reflected in Israel's Knesset (Israel's Parliament). In America, we have over 300 million differing opinions. That is how the system of capitalism works. So why only have two opinions in Congress when we can have three? Why not have a Government that reflects more the diverse voices of capitalism in its own halls of Congress?

Conclusion

In this book, I spoke of the need for a third political party, which I tentatively call the moderately centrist party. I spoke of my wavering political opinions throughout the years. I then gave real world examples of how political leaders can be moderate and how I myself am moderate. And I spoke passionately about how a third party would reflect the values of innovation and capitalism by raising the number of voices in Congress from two differing viewpoints to three.

Preface To Kuwait, Qatar, And Israel

While I did serve in the U.S. Army, I did not see combat. I say again, I did not see combat. In fact, the highlight of my Army career was a year-long deployment in Kuwait in support of Operation Iraqi Freedom as an Administrative Specialist who typed on a computer all day. While in Kuwait, I visited Qatar, and after my Kuwait deployment, I went on a religious mission to Israel. After all of this, I finished my Bachelor's Degree in Political Science and worked several civilian jobs. I will spend most of this book speaking about my time in Kuwait, Qatar, and Israel, and how that shaped my views on Middle East Peace.

Chapter 1: Enlisting In The U.S. Army

When I was very young, my family bought me a book about ancient Egypt. I was fascinated by the history in it. The story of the Egyptian Dynasties, the stories of the Pharaohs, and the stories of the Pyramids inspired me. I did not know that several decades later, when I was all grown up, that the Middle East would become my number one passion in life. I will now flash forward to my High School days. In the 2002-2003 school year, towards the end of High School, I went to my gym teacher, a man whom to this day I have great respect for, and told him I want to prepare for the Army. He told me I should wrestle. The workouts were difficult, and I lost a lot of weight; I went down from 200 lbs. all the way to 152 lbs. at one point. I got to meet a lot of good people on the team and I even got to wrestle at two tournaments. My school had one of the greatest Wrestling teams in my state. Thank goodness I decided to wrestle before I joined the Army as Basic Combat Training would be the most grueling physical training I have ever done in my life to this day. And wrestling definitely prepared me for that and got me in good shape.

During the first Wrestling tournament, I wrestled a 6'3" inch tall white gentleman with blonde hair and blue eyes. His hair was long, about almost up to the shoulders and very curly. We wrestled at 171 lbs., even though the gentleman was much taller and much bigger than me. I am only 5'7". I was not too nervous though. I was just thinking, *I am going to stay in this thing as long as I can. I am not going for the pin but I am going to wrestle for as long as I can.* When the whistle was blown, I came in very quickly and locked up with one arm around his shoulder and the other arm around the back of his neck.

I was very inexperienced, so my tactic was to try to scare him. In hindsight, it was a bad idea to try to scare someone who is 6'3" and 171 lbs. of solid muscle. I began to push and pull him again and again in an effort to both off-balance and intimidate him. Then I went for a single leg. A single leg in Wrestling is when you move forward and bend down a little and grab one leg of the opponent. You then either trip his other leg with your own leg or you go for what is known as a double leg. A double leg is when you grab one leg and then grab the second leg and go down with him. Note that in Folkstyle High School Wrestling, you cannot throw your opponent to the floor without going down with him to secure his landing, because that would be known as a slam.

Anyhow, he ended up doing a body lock on me. A move that I have not learned yet. I tried to bend down slightly and shoot for his leg (move quickly towards him and then slide on one knee in his direction). He grabbed me in a type of bear hug from the front and then transitioned to standing behind me while still holding me and tossed me and went down with me of course to secure my landing. But it felt like the black rubber mat was made out of concrete when I hit it. He even took the wind out of me when I hit the mat and I remember my wrestling singlet, a one piece wrestling uniform that we wore with special wrestling shoes, being covered completely in sweat within two to three seconds of me hitting the mat. His arms were still wrapped around me and he was holding his hands tightly together around my stomach area. I grabbed for his hands and tried to pry them off, but then, using his superior strength and technique, he proceeded to put me on the mat on my back and pin me and I struggled at first, but his hold was so strong that I eventually gave up and just laid there until the referee blew the whistle. Afterwards, we all went through a line (one team made one line and the other team made another line) and we went by and thanked each other. Either the gentleman I wrestled or someone that looks very similar to him, stated to me, as he shook my hand, "Way to wrestle." He knew I had heart.

The 2nd gentleman I wrestled was a white gentleman, with a blonde buzz cut, weighed about 152 lbs. and was about 5'6", an inch shorter than me. This was at my 2nd Wrestling tournament, a few weeks later. Even though the gentleman was an inch shorter than me, my one inch height advantage was negated by the fact that I lost so much weight to compete against him. At 171 lbs., I had already learned my lesson to not wrestle guys who are too heavy for me, as their muscle overrides my fat. So coming in this time at 152 lbs., I did a little bit better. I got out of some of his holds, which surprised me as he was very fast, and I lasted into the 2nd round, but he eventually pinned me. While not as strong as my previous opponent, he felt twice as fast. At the Wrestling tournaments, I lost both matches that I wrestled but I, and everyone else on the team, knew I had heart. This heart I would need to make it through Army Basic Training.

I graduated from High School in May of 2003 and enlisted in the U.S. Army Reserve. After attending a few drills with my Army Reserve unit, whom would become some of the greatest people I've ever known, I attended Basic Combat Training at Ft. Jackson, South Carolina. I left for Basic Combat Training on November 4th, 2003.

The Drill Sergeants were hard but fair. They were also some of the greatest people I've ever known. I want to get this off my chest. My scariest moments were Victory Tower and the Confidence Course.

I am scared of heights. I remember being told by my fellow recruits to have discipline and look straight ahead while getting ready to go up Victory Tower, a 30 foot massive behemoth, complete with a repelling wall, a ropes course, and a cargo net. They told me this as per the instructions of the Drill Sergeants there. We were to stand at attention while waiting in line, but I was so scared that I could not help but look up at the looming tower. I went up and down the tower, went through the ropes course, and went down the cargo net. I did all these things, but I forgot which order I did them in. It wasn't as scary as I thought it would be, but scary nonetheless.

My second scariest moment was the Confidence Course. I remember being really scared going up the giant ladder, which, like Victory Tower, was also 30 feet high. I was scared, but once again, I did it. That is all I remember from the Confidence Course, other than the fact that it rained and we had to cancel the rest of the course after I completed about half of it. I am sure glad that I made it through both Victory Tower and The Confidence Course, I consider those two events in particular, and making it through Basic Combat Training in general, two of some of my biggest accomplishments in life.

Another event that I remember was the Gas Chamber. I remember being told before going to Basic

Training by some Veterans and Active Duty military alike to not shave beforehand and to not eat the Chili Mac that the Drill Sergeants will offer you. I enjoyed some of the food that the Drill Sergeants served us but I did not eat the Chili Mac as it was not a requirement but I did shave beforehand, as I consider myself very "Hooah!" Hooah is a word in the Army that means everything but 'no'. As we lined up in the Gas Chamber, around the Dragon (the cauldron that emitted the CS Gas), I remembered that we were told by the Drill Sergeant to not touch the Dragon. By this point, we were all wearing our Protective Masks.

In the Army, you call them Protective Masks and not Gas Masks; this was a requirement just as calling your rifle a weapon and not a gun was also a requirement. The Drill Sergeants were obviously wearing the Protective Masks too as they came into the Gas Chamber well before we did. Then we were told to take our hand and put it on the lower part of our masks and move them up, just enough to inhale some CS gas, say Name, Rank, and Social Security Number, as well as sing The Army Song. I said all this in between screaming from the pain of the CS getting into the pores of my face. Everyone else tended to cough a lot. I regretted shaving that morning.

After singing and saying my pertinent data, we were told to put the bottom part of the masks back on and clear and seal the masks. I cleared the mask with my right hand while breathing out and then I put my left hand on the filter and breathed in until the mask stuck to my face. I then released my left hand and the mask unstuck from my face. You know your mask is sealed when putting your hand on the filter and breathing in makes the mask stick to your face. We were then told to remove our masks completely, sing The Army Song, and then leave the Gas Chamber. As scary as the Gas Chamber is for some recruits, it was not scary for me as being in an enclosed environment low to the ground means I won't have to deal with heights, one of my biggest fears, and my only irrational phobia.

I must apologize for discussing my Basic Training experience in an out of order fashion as I am remembering the most interesting parts first. On the Rifle Qualification Range, on my 2nd attempt, I made Marksman. While the lowest qualification score, I was happy with it as I made the standard and was on my way to graduate Basic Training. My biggest challenge, passing the Two-Mile Run in under sixteen minutes and thirty six seconds, was yet to come.

My favorite part of Basic Combat Training was the Anzio Range, named after a World War II Battle that took place in Italy. We went navigating through pitch black, at nighttime, and I could barely see, and eventually all of us (the recruits) got to a set of metal pole stakes towards the end of the course. Each set of stakes contained two stakes, one on each side of the recruit's weapon. They were placed in sectors of fire. A sector of fire is where a Soldier is ordered to visually scan the landscape/terrain in front of him/her, and if need be, fire his/her weapon at the enemy.

As I got to my sector of fire, I got in the prone position and readied my M16A2 rifle. I took it off Safe and put it on Semi and began to fire. I neglected to mention that we had tracer rounds in our magazine. So, I don't remember exactly if every round was a tracer round, or if every third or fourth round was a tracer round, but our M16 rifles lit up the night. They looked like short laser beams from science fiction movies. Not only did I experience awe that night, I also achieved my training objectives for the evening.

Chapter 2: The Dreaded 2 Mile Run And Victory Forge

On the day of the 2 Mile Run, my Drill Sergeant had one of the most high speed (quick-learning) and squared away (knows what needs to be done and how to do it) Soldiers run alongside with me. I passed the Pushups and Situps on the APFT (Army Physical Fitness Test) with no problems. Then as I ran, even at sea level at Ft. Jackson, I remember screaming from the pain in my chest and pain in my legs as I have never ran so hard in my life. The recruit, a six foot two inch tall blonde gentleman with blue eyes, who was wearing a gray Army PT (physical training) T-shirt and black Army shorts, white socks, and white sneakers, as was I, ran alongside me.

The Drill Sergeant who was watching our progress stood near the middle of the oval-shaped track we were running on. We were running outdoors. During the test, I could hear various music from 70's, 80's, and 90's action and sports movies playing to get us pumped up. I ran hard and fast, sometimes screaming as loud as I can. This was both from the pain and to open up my diaphragm and increase my rate of breathing. Running as hard and as fast as I could, I managed to pass the test in 15:48; the required test time minimum was 16:36. I barely made it, but what mattered was that I *did* make it.

The next day came Victory Forge. We put on our BDUs (Battle Dress Uniforms), what civilians call green woodland camouflage uniforms. We got our LBV (load-bearing vests) on. The LBV is basically a green vest that goes over the uniform that carries a first aid pouch and pouches for extra magazines for the M16 rifle. We also put on our Kevlar helmets. The Kevlar helmets had bands that we put in to make wearing them more comfortable, nevertheless it became uncomfortable very quickly during the march as both the headband became tight and the helmet became heavy. We also wore a rucksack which carried additional gear. I remember the 1st generation rucksacks being hard to tie up after we filled them up and being almost as hard to put on. We carried our M16 rifles during the 10 mile march.

Marching was easy as I am a good walker, but not a good runner. I made it all 10 miles to the site of Victory Forge, our FTX (Field Training Exercise), without getting tired. I was moving so fast and it came so naturally and easily for me that my Drill Sergeant said something to me I thought I would never hear, "Slow down." Even the high speed gentleman that helped me run said he never thought that he would hear the Drill Sergeant say that.

The site of Victory Forge was a heavily wooded area of Ft. Jackson. It looked like it was straight out of a World War II movie. We began to dig our trenches. I do not remember if we used actual shovels, an entrenching tool, or both, but we dug and dug, and after about a day, my Battle Buddy and I had dug a two person trench, as had everyone else in our Basic Training Platoon (a platoon is a 30 person unit). An entrenching tool is like a sharp small shovel that can either dig a trench or be used to attack an enemy, much like a bayonet. A battle buddy is a person who is part of your two person team in Basic Training. You never go anywhere without a battle buddy, who is always your same rank (I was a Private at the time). We also had two person tents that we set up.

The fact that my Basic Training was in the winter time was both a blessing and a curse. A blessing in that it was very unusually cold and easy to run and march in, but a curse in that I only slept one hour in all of the seventy-two hours we were out there at Victory Forge, because of the cold. We finished digging our trenches during the day, and at night came our first simulated enemy attack during Victory Forge. A flare shot up in the sky and the night, for several seconds, became illuminated almost like daytime. We heard blank ammunition going off and several CS grenades were thrown towards us. So we naturally put on our protective masks and yelled, "Gas! Gas! Gas!" We stood in our trenches, waiting for the simulated enemy attack. Then came the CS grenades. It's amazing, I was coughing until I put on my mask, but the Drill Sergeants were walking around without masks and the CS did not seem to affect them. At one point, one of the Drill Sergeants commented that my weapon (M16A2 rifle) was frosted over when he came over to inspect our trench after the simulated gas attack.

After two and a half days, we started the long march back. Back in the Barracks, I was so tired from only sleeping one hour during that whole period that I felt refreshed after sleeping four to five hours in the Barracks. The next day was graduation. We got in our Class A uniforms (that is a Green Military Dress Suit uniform) and attended graduation. We heard the Colonel and then General speak and we sang the Army Song. Basic Training was hard but I do miss my Drill Sergeants and feel that it was one of my favorite times of my life. I got my Orders for AIT (Advanced Individualized Training, or job training), in the front leaning rest (pushup) position.

Chapter 3: AIT

This will be a short chapter as I call this next part Basic Training Lite. Since my MOS (Military Occupational Specialty) was as an Administrative Specialist, a support MOS with training at Ft. Jackson, I did not have to go far for AIT (Advanced Individualized Training). We got on a bus and were bussed from one part of the base to another. Our Drill Sergeants and the Sergeants that trained us for our MOS at AIT were more relaxed and I felt less jacked up (more able to handle this and not as physically slow as I was in Basic Training). It really helped that my High School Business teacher taught me how to type home row. I ended up typing over 80 words per minute in High School. This only helped me at AIT. We did a lot of typing of reports and we concluded with a field exercise, with a slightly shorter march and slightly shorter time in the field. Thankfully, AIT was very easy and like I said in the beginning of the chapter, it was basically Basic Training Lite.

I was glad it was easier with less marching and less time in the field as we were in the month of February at AIT and it was starting to get hot in South Carolina. So maybe it was a blessing in disguise that it was unusually cold when I got to Basic Combat Training. After I completed my Admin training, this was now early 2004, I got back to my unit and spent some time stationed on a base on active duty stateside. Then after I finished my stateside tour, I went to University concurrently with my Army Reserve training. I studied Political Science. After a year of school, I got called up to Active Duty again. This time to Kuwait.

Chapter 4: Kuwait

Around August of 2005, my unit and I arrived at Ft. Bliss, Texas. We then did three months of training before deploying to Kuwait. I remember we had convoy training. Lots and lots of convoy training with Humvees. After we finished training and got our paperwork squared away, we boarded a plane and after what seemed like half a day of flying, landed in Kuwait. We landed in Kuwait on November 4th, 2005. This was coincidentally two years to the day that I left for Basic Training. After we arrived on base, it felt very cool and nice. Not too hot and not too cold. We stayed in temporary housing tents that fit about ten people each for the first several weeks of our deployment. Then we were moved to our trailers that we would call home for the rest of the deployment. After a few months on base, the contractors on base turned on the AC. We were complaining for two days that it was too cold and that they turned on the AC too early. We would soon realize how wrong we were too complain as soon the temperature got up to 110 Degrees Fahrenheit, and eventually, in June, July, and August of 2006, the temperature got up to 127 Degrees Fahrenheit in the shaded area, even though all our thermometers actually read 140 Degrees and over in Fahrenheit. I will not spend any more time talking about what I did military-wise in Kuwait, other than I did Admin work, but I will tell you about life there and the people and their beautiful culture that I experienced.

I remember visiting Kuwait City. They have a beautiful pier there that overlooks antique boats. They have a cultural center there too. There were several beautiful skyscrapers there as well. Most of the country is contrasted with two story tall buildings made out of concrete. Only Kuwait City, as far as I know, had the skyscrapers. This is similar to Israel, in how Tel Aviv has many skyscrapers and West Jerusalem has several skyscrapers, but the rest of the country has smaller buildings. But I will get into Israel in the chapter after the next one. I remember eating at a Kuwaiti restaurant. We ate a marvelous rice dish and the servers and hosts were very pleasant, warm, and friendly.

The animal life was beautiful too, and in my mind, very unique. When I went to a museum/zoo in Kuwait City, the cats were tan and had pointed ears like the elves from early folklore. The rats had forward bent knees and jump up and down like kangaroos, hence their name, kangaroo rats. There were camels, and then there were scorpions and camel spiders. The camel spider is like a large tan-colored and very hairy spider, but not poisonous, at least, I don't think. The scorpions are the ones that people should worry about. But like we were told stateside when several Soldiers inquired about mosquitos, there are no mosquitos in the Middle East. Thank goodness. But there are locusts.

And I remember in the fall (both in November 2005 and October 2006), on base, we had literally a Biblical-proportion plague of locusts. I was literally walking around one time and I had hundreds of locusts all over me and all around me, but they seemed, and were, very harmless. The sight of them was more beautiful than anything else. Also on base, I remember there were entire weeks when we would see a giant blood orange moon. I don't know why it was so big, but it looked three or four times bigger than what the moon looks like back home in the United States. Looking back on it now, I am thinking that the Kuwaiti moonlight should be called one of the wonders of the world.

And then, then came the dreaded PT Test again. This was sometime in mid-2006, don't remember when exactly. This time, I had to make it in 15:54. I was a Private First Class at the time. A Staff Sergeant with my unit, a 5'7" black gentleman, who had a slight accent, and was always ready to help anyone who ever needed it, ran alongside me. I have a slight accent too, being originally from Ukraine. He kept yelling at me to, "Hurry up. Get here. Get right here!" and he pointed to where he wanted me to be at. I struggled to keep up, I ran so fast, and screamed and yelled and was in so much pain. But I had to keep up. *I cannot let myself fail*, I thought.

I was told after the test ended, in which I ran a 15:50 and passed, that I kept up with one of the fastest people in the unit, a gentleman originally from Belarus. One gentleman in my unit even commented that he thought I was a monster coming to eat him when I was running because I was yelling so much. I guess I do have heart. I then got my promotion to my final rank of Specialist. A Specialist is the same pay grade as Corporal, but with less command responsibility. That became one of my proudest achievements in the Army. I will always remember what that Staff Sergeant did for me to make this happen. After the PT Test, came my R&R pass to Qatar. I had so much fun in Qatar.

Chapter 5: Qatar

This, the R&R Pass to Qatar, was also in mid-2006, like the PT Test. On my 4 day R&R pass, I stayed on a really cool base in Qatar. We had pizza, three beers a day, and TV. I normally don't drink, I drink hardly ever, but I did end up having three beers a day every night. On the first day, I went off-roading with several other Soldiers in an SUV. The Qatari driver took us up to the top of the sand dunes, one sand dune at a time, obviously, and then took us straight down. It was very fast and very cool. I even have grainy video of us going down the sand dunes to this day. On the second day, I went to several restaurants.

The people who served us were very nice and very friendly. At one restaurant, which overlooked the Persian Gulf, the gentleman who owned it, said many people go to this restaurant from all over the Middle East. Some that go are Syrian, some Palestinian, and some are Jordanian, among others. I remember going to a Hookah bar in Qatar and smoking tobacco through a Hookah pipe. I am a tobacco user, both smoker and chewer, so I loved the Hookah bar. Then I went with several other Soldiers to the beach. Now I can say to people I've been to the Persian Gulf.

On the third day, I went to the mall. I met a very friendly Egyptian gentleman that really hooked me up. He showed me around the mall and even let me smoke cigarettes with him, even indoors! That used to be legal here in the United States but now, unfortunately for me, it is now illegal. Smoking sections of restaurants are now nonexistent. He showed me some of the shops, where the local shopkeepers were so nice. I purchased several Egyptian-style pyramids made out of stone, about hand-held sized. I purchased a scorpion and camel spider encased in acrylic. I also purchased several Russian-style Matryoshka dolls. The Matryoshka dolls were especially cool, since I'm originally from Ukraine, they remind me of my heritage.

I remember feeling very sad that I did not take many pictures of my time in Qatar. When the Egyptian gentleman I was with asked me why I looked sad, I stated that I did not have anything to remember this place by. So he took pictures of me with Hookah pipes at the Hookah store, he took pictures of me with paintings, and he took pictures of me with Egyptian statues that were in the mall.

I just remembered that I have pictures of myself with a red hat with a tassel on it, called a Fez. The gentleman I spoke of took those pictures too. I don't know the origin of it, but it could be generally Middle Eastern or specifically Moroccan, I am not sure though. We even listened to Rap and R&B music together. I miss hanging out with him. On the fourth day in Qatar, I remember having my three beers, ordering a large pizza, and watching a horror movie on TV. I must have ate that entire pizza in less than five minutes because I was so hungry. After I got back from Qatar to Kuwait, our deployment was wrapping up.

Chapter 6: Heading Home

In October of 2006, as the bus was leaving the base, and was taking us to the airport, a tear welled up in my eye as I would miss everyone that I worked with, the U.S. Military Servicemembers and the contractors. Our plane left Kuwait and after several stops in Europe, we landed stateside. Back home, my family was very happy to see me. I was happy to see them too. I spent almost twelve months deployed in Kuwait.

I was back on Reserve status after my deployment. I then started finishing up my University studies in Political Science. We were scheduled to do Annual Training in California, but I asked my Sergeant, Staff Sergeant, and Commander (a Captain at the time) if I could instead go on a Jewish religious mission to Israel, which my family had planned. The Commander authorized it. So now, I am back home, in school full-time, and planning a trip to Israel.

Chapter 7: Israel

I attended a Jewish religious mission in Israel in the summer of 2007. We landed in Tel Aviv and our tour guides picked us up, along with them, was a Rabbi. I am remembering now that we once went on a tour of King Solomon's aqueducts in East Jerusalem. We were underground and there was water up to our knees. It was fun though and it was an honor to do it. We prayed at the Wailing Wall, also in East Jerusalem. While I am secular now, I definitely remember feeling a tie to God and His presence when I was putting my note in the wall and saying a prayer as well. We went hiking a lot. We hiked on the Golan Heights one time. It was beautiful seeing the true beauty of nature. I have never hiked before until I visited Israel. When we visited Tel Aviv, I saw how different it looked from the rest of Israel. It had a bunch of steel skyscrapers while the rest of the country had concrete buildings. Very similar to how Kuwait had many concrete buildings and Kuwait City had a bunch of steel skyscrapers.

We went to several bars in Tel Aviv and after one or two nights of hiking and going sightseeing, I stopped going to bars and drinking. Even after two shots of Vodka, I felt too tired to go hiking and traveling the next day, but did so anyway, and to keep from being tired anymore while doing it, I just stayed in my hotel room at nighttime. By the way, in Israel a shot of Vodka is known as a chaser of Vodka, and two shots of Vodka are known as a shot of Vodka, if that makes sense. While in my hotel room, I listened to Israeli Hip Hop, Rock, R&B, Pop, and Mizrahi music that I purchased at the mall when we went to the mall in Tel Aviv. Israeli Mizrahi music, Mizrahi meaning 'Eastern' in Hebrew, sounds like Arabic music. In fact, many people who don't speak Arabic or Hebrew cannot distinguish Israeli or Arabic music from each other. That is how similar they are. I will speak of further cultural similarities between Israeli people and Arab people in future chapters.

My favorite experience, next to the Wailing Wall, of course, was going up the Fortress of Masada. You can see much of Israel from the top of there. The Masada Fortress was where a group of Ancient Israelites ran upon each other's swords rather than surrender to the invading Romans. Another equally favorite experience, just as good as seeing Masada, was spending the night at a Bedouin tent. The Bedouins are a group of nomadic Arabs who live in Israel. They gave us tea and food and let us stay in their tent for a night. They are a very humble and generous people. At one point during our trip in Israel, we even got to ride camels. I've ridden them before, stateside, at a Medieval Festival, but it is so much more powerful when you do it in the Middle East.

Chapter 8: My Future Plans

After I returned home from Israel, I gave my family some Israeli music CDs that I bought in Israel. You see, I bought multiple copies, some for myself, and some for family. By the way, just as Hebrew and Arabic are written right to left, Israeli music CD cases open in the opposite direction too. I then finished up my Bachelor's Degree in Political Science at University and finished up my military service with the U.S. Army Reserve, both in 2008. I worked several civilian jobs, from 2010-2018, and like in the military, the civilians I worked with became like family too, after several years of working with them. At University, like in Kuwait, Qatar, and Israel, I met many Jewish and Israeli students and professors, as well as Palestinian students and professors. They were very nice.

At my civilian jobs, I have met several Israeli and Palestinian customers and employees who were equally as kind as those that I met at University.

Now I want to speak about what I want to do with my life next. I know it sounds like an ambitious goal, but I want to make the world a better place. I may make it a career in helping to shape the Middle East for a brighter future, but for now, I want this book to help the reader see what I think should happen in the Middle East. With my life experience in the Military, having served in Kuwait and having visited Qatar, and with my Jewish religious mission in Israel, and with my Political Science Degree, I know that I pretty much have a calling to work towards a better Middle East.

Chapter 9: A Top-Down Approach To Middle East Peace

Governments in Israel and in the Arab World are currently working toward Middle East Peace. We have heard of the One State Solution. In the One State Solution, we would have one state encompassing the whole Israeli-Palestinian peninsula for both the Israelis and Palestinians.

We have heard of the Two-State Solution. The Two-State Solution involves Gaza and the West Bank becoming part of Palestine while pre-1967 Israel would stay as part of Israel. This is all good. As I write this, Saudi Arabia and Israel are developing a closer relationship in dealing with common security issues. The Israelis and Palestinians work in the Jordan Valley together on water rights, as well as on economic issues that affect both their peoples throughout the Israeli-Palestinian peninsula. Again, this is all good.

Governments need to continue to work for Middle East Peace. The U.N. and the U.S. should stay involved in the Middle East Peace Process as well. This is all working towards a good goal. But this is only the Top-Down Approach to Middle East Peace. I recommend, in addition to the Top-Down Approach, a Bottom-Up Approach to Middle East Peace.

Chapter 10: A Bottom-Up Approach To Middle East Peace

As I said in Chapter 8, my Kuwait deployment and my trip to Israel, as well as studying Political Science at University, has made me passionate about the Middle East and helping the people living there. In Kuwait and Qatar, as well as during my stay at the Bedouin tent in Israel, I learned first-hand about the friendliness and hospitality of the Arab people. They were willing to help me out when I needed help by taking photographs of me in Qatar when I had very few deployment photographs. They offered me free food and drink. And they took me on tours and listened to music with me. The Israeli people were equally kind. They taught me about Israeli culture and taught me about my Jewish heritage and took me all over the country to see what Israel is like.

I feel that, like how Governments work together for Middle East Peace, the people should work together for Middle East Peace too. As the people of Kuwait, Qatar, and Israel have been kind to me, I feel I need to repay that kindness by helping foster peace. For the remainder of this book, I will focus on the Israeli-Palestinian Peace Process for two reasons. 1.) It is very crucial to the entire region. And 2.) I studied it the most while in University.

In the United States, there are probably a hundred to two hundred Middle East Peace NGOs and Nonprofit Groups. And maybe ten to twenty large Middle East Peace NGOs and Nonprofit Groups functioning as umbrella organizations. I feel that there should be a thousand to five thousand Middle East Peace NGOs and Nonprofit Groups and maybe two hundred to three hundred large umbrella Middle East Peace NGOs and Nonprofit Groups.

In Israel and as well as in Kuwait and Qatar, I saw that both the Jewish People and the Arab People all have the same mannerisms. They all have the same hand gestures. They all have the same facial mannerisms. They even have a very similar inflection in language and speaking. They both speak Semitic languages (Arabic and Hebrew). Like I said earlier in the book, Arabic music and Israeli Mizrahi (Eastern) music both sound similar. And about half of classical Jewish music, if not more than half, sounds just as Middle Eastern as Arabic music. They both worship the same God as well.

We need to bring regular, everyday people from Israel and Palestine together on a massive scale the way we bring the Governments together. I know creating more NGOs costs money, but at the same time, if we give people the chance to see they have more in common than they thought, then I feel that this financial price is a price worth paying. If everyone in the Middle East just took a day of their lives to meet someone who is slightly different than them in some ways, but very similar in others, and took the time to talk to them, they would see that they are brothers and sisters and not adversaries.

Like I said before, in addition to Governments working together for peace, another commonly neglected path to peace is to have the people come together and talk. This is what is now needed to supplement the Peace Process. And hopefully, it will supplement the Peace Process to a great extent. Also, I have to note, in addition to finding common ground between Israelis and Palestinians, I always challenge myself to find one thing that I and somebody else like. Everyone is passionate about at least one thing that someone else that may be somehow different than them may be equally passionate about. That is what I strive for. And that is what we need to strive for in making peace.

Chapter 11: The Best Of Both Worlds And Finding One Commonality

Having introduced my bottom-up approach to peace, and having spoken of the already existing top-down approach to peace, I feel that it is critical for peace to succeed by having what I call the best of both worlds approach to peace. We need to have Middle Eastern Governments continue to have security cooperation and financial cooperation. But the people need to speak to each other too. That is why I think in the Middle East and in the United States, both the private sector and the government (Federal, State, and Local) should encourage the growth of more peace NGOs and Nonprofits by simply speaking about them. The funding will come later as more people decide to speak out by speaking to each other. When people see there is a demand for more peace and development organizations, then the funding will come.

When these new NGOs bring people together, even if the people meeting feel they have too many differences, the NGO should speak to them about finding one thing they are both passionate about. This one thing is what will unite those two individuals in their new bond. They will then not only help bring about Middle East Peace but will also use that one thing they have in common to create change for the better in other ways as well. This one commonality approach can bring about Middle East Peace from the bottom up, with some help from the top down. Governments will continue to negotiate and people will continue to speak with each other, and within a decade or so, we may very well have a lasting peace.

Chapter 12: The Committee Of Commonalities

Whether one supports a One State Solution or a Two-State Solution, I do not believe that the Israeli-Palestinian conflict is unsolvable. We as a society have been looking at the differences between Israelis and Palestinians, both politically and culturally, for decades now, and we should start looking at the similarities. The U.S. Government, the U.N., NATO Countries, the Arab League, and the Israelis and Palestinians should work together to create a joint Israeli-Palestinian Committee Of Commonalities. This committee will be staffed by both Israelis and Palestinians. They will do research on what common cultural and political interests both sides have. They will then use this to create a just Israeli-Palestinian peace.

The Committee Of Commonalities will be staffed by both Government Officials and Private Citizens, thus combining the top down and bottom up approach. It will host foreign dignitaries who will advise the Israelis and Palestinians on how to adapt the security procedures of their own countries to Israel and Palestine, and guest speakers such as U.S. Military Active Duty and Veterans (both Officers and Enlisted) will further advise the Committee Of Commonalities as to security procedures. Everyday Israelis and Palestinians will advise The Committee Of Commonalities of the cultural sensitivities of both sides and both sides will learn to value and respect those sensitivities. Political Members of The Committee Of Commonalities will map out a just peace that both sides can agree with based on both differences and similarities, with the key focus being similarities.

Chapter 13: The NGOs Of Commonalities

Just as we should have an Israeli-Palestinian Committee Of Commonalities in the Government sphere that will combine both private citizens and government officials, we should also have NGOs that work on commonalities on the ground level. We already have NGOs in the United States that bring Israelis and Palestinians together, and this is good. I support expanding this. Like I said earlier in this book, by twice as much, three times as much, or even ten times as much. We need Israelis and Palestinians to meet more often. More private individuals meeting and speaking of peaceful brotherhood and sisterhood will allow for them to make change for the better. We need to create NGOs of Commonalities as well. By speaking out about their commonalities, Israelis and Palestinians can help bring about peace. Many Israelis and Palestinians that meet may like the same type of music. They may like Mixed Martial Arts. They may like Science Fiction. Whatever their hobbies, dreams, goals, they (Israelis and Palestinians) can learn to pursue them together.

  While working together at the NGO level, to meet as friends and to speak to each other, and discuss their commonalities, or at least one big commonality, they can help bring about change at the local level, and eventually, they can petition the Israeli and Palestinian Governments, as well as the U.S. Government, of the necessary needs for change. The people should speak to the government and the government should then speak to the people. This way, everyone's views will be heard and not just the elite or those in political power. By speaking to each other, these NGOs of Commonalities and the Israeli-Palestinian Committee Of Commonalities can advise their local community as well as the Israeli and Palestinian Governments at the federal level of the need for a peaceful solution to the Israeli-Palestinian Conflict.

Chapter 14: A Realistic Two-State Solution

I do have to apologize beforehand as I will not discuss the Golan Heights as it is a matter between Israel and Syria, and I am less familiar with Syria. I will though discuss the West Bank and pre-1967 Israel as it pertains to both the Israelis and Palestinians, a subject I know much about and am passionate about. What is pre-1967 Israel? During the Six Day War of June 1967, Israel ended up winning a war against Egypt, Syria, and Jordan. Israel came out of that war with its original borders, at least the post-1948 borders (the War Of Independence for Israel was in 1948), along with the military gains of Gaza from Egypt, East Jerusalem and the West Bank from Jordan, the Golan Heights from Syria, and the Sinai Peninsula, which was also from Egypt. Israel withdrew from the Sinai Peninsula in 1982 and gave it back to Egypt, in exchange for a Peace Treaty. Israel withdrew from Gaza in 2005.

I support what I call a realistic Two-State Solution. Israel would withdraw from The West Bank, while East Jerusalem would become a joint capitol for the Israelis and Palestinians. The West Bank and Gaza would fall under complete Palestinian control. Regular Israeli bus and Israeli train service would help Palestinians go from Gaza to the West Bank and vice versa, with Israeli military and Israeli police protecting the busses and trains. East Jerusalem's Muslim quarter would be part of the capitol of

Palestine, and the Jewish quarter would become part of the capital of Israel. Israelis who wish to remain in the West Bank would be considered Israeli Citizens living abroad in the country of Palestine, while Palestinians who wish to reside in Israel would be considered Citizens of Palestine living abroad in Israel. The Muslim quarter of East Jerusalem, while being part of the capital of Palestine, would be staffed by both Israeli Muslims and Palestinian Muslims, as a way to show friendship and peace. The Jewish quarter would be staffed by Israeli Jews from Israel. The Christian quarter would be staffed by Israeli Christians and Palestinian Christians and would be split between Israel and Palestine, in terms of responsibility. And the Armenian quarter would be staffed by Armenians, with the Armenians deciding whether they want their quarter to be part of Israel, Palestine, or both.

I feel that this is the most realistic solution to the issue at hand. Israel and Palestine would coordinate water usage in the Jordan Valley, which would be under Palestinian control, in exchange for Israel offering technological innovations and gas from offshore off of Israel's coast near the city of Haifa. In addition to having a realistic Two-State Solution, Israel would have an embassy in the original capital of Palestine, Ramallah, and Palestine would have an embassy in the Israeli city of Tel Aviv. This would lead to full diplomatic relations. After full diplomatic relations are created between Israel and Palestine, other Arab nations will follow Palestine's suit and start establishing relations with Israel. The Governmental relations between Israel and Palestine will also lead to security cooperation, which will be discussed in the two chapters after the next one.

Chapter 15: A Fair Compromise For Israel and Palestine

In exchange for agreeing to the Two-State Solution, the United States should give Palestine several M1A1 Abrams tanks, several armored Humvees, and several transport helicopters as well as Apache attack helicopters. This will help Palestine with future security needs and will help it work as part of a Middle Eastern version of NATO, which will help the Middle East as a whole. To keep its quantitative and qualitative edge in the Middle East, in exchange for agreeing to the Two-State Solution, the United States should give Israel two Los Angeles Class Attack Submarines to replace two of their German-built diesel submarines. The U.S. should also give Israel ten F-22 fighter jets to replace ten of their aging F-16 fighter jets. Israel and Palestine can then coordinate security activities together while part of a peace pact which will lead to a Middle Eastern version of NATO, to be discussed in the next chapter.

Chapter 16: A Middle Eastern Version Of NATO

In the First World War, we had the Allied Powers and the Central Powers. The Allied Powers, led by France, Great Britain, and the United States, defeated the Central Powers. Then came World War II. In the Second World War, we had the Allies and the Axis Powers. After the defeat of Nazi Germany by the Allies, led by The U.S., Great Britain, and the Soviet Union, and the defeat of Japan, the Cold War came about with the Soviet Union on one side and The United States and NATO (North Atlantic Treaty Organization) on the other side. Even after the end of the Cold War and the fall of the Berlin Wall, NATO remained in place.

I feel that the relationship between the U.S and NATO is strong and NATO countries have helped the U.S. greatly, with countries like Great Britain, Germany, among others, helping us out in the War On Terrorism. I have to say that the NATO system works well. That is why I am proposing a Middle Eastern version of NATO.

Starting with what I call the IPCISO (Israeli-Palestinian Counterterrorism and Intelligence Sharing Organization). It can be either an Office within the Senior Staff of Israeli and Palestinian Military and Government or it can be a joint unit, Special Operations or Regular

Military, of the Israeli Defense Force and the Palestinian security organizations. This Office will eventually grow to form a joint Military-wide unit of Israelis and Palestinians. What I mean is this will be a two country Middle Eastern NATO. After a Peace Process deal is finalized, or even before, this Middle Eastern version of NATO may one day become greater in scope, encompassing some, most, or all of the Middle East.

Chapter 17: NASWAA

The name is not as important as the function, but I would personally name the new NATO of the Middle East as the North African-Southwest Asian Alliance (NASWAA). They would coordinate security-related issues with not only with each other in the Middle East, but with NATO and the United States. NASWAA would deploy troops throughout the Middle East to deal with terrorism-related incidents and perhaps to keep the peace as well. They would also, with approval of NATO and the U.S., for the first time, deploy outside the Middle East to help with any tensions outside the region, while partnered with NATO.

Through cooperation between countries such as Morocco, Tunisia, Libya, Algeria, Egypt, Saudi Arabia, Oman, Yemen, Qatar, Bahrain, United Arab Emirates, Turkey, Israel and Palestine, among others, these countries will work with NATO and the U.S. for security not only in the Middle East, but around the world. This would give the countries of the Middle East more presence on the world stage which would be a morale booster to their people, in my opinion. The people of these countries will feel more valued if they have more of an impact on a global level.

This will probably not come to fruition for another ten or twenty years from when I am writing this book (in 2018). We may not have a Middle Eastern NATO just yet, but we can achieve Israeli and Palestinian peace and have an Israeli-Palestinian IPCISO (Israeli-Palestinian Counterterrorism and Intelligence Sharing Organization), which will of course serve as a forerunner to the new NASWAA (North African-Southwest Asian Alliance).

Chapter 18: What It All Means

What I have now proposed in the last few chapters is a Two-State Solution, followed by more military aid for both a smaller and more secure Israel and a smaller and more secure Palestine. I have also proposed the North African-Southwest Asian Alliance, a Middle Eastern version of NATO. Once the Israelis and Palestinians have peace, and Israel is given a slight qualitative and quantitative edge for security purposes, and Palestine is given more military aid for its own internal security, they can work on security cooperation. They can work on counterterrorism operations together, they can work on intelligence sharing, and they can work on what their vision of a Middle Eastern NATO would look like.

As I am writing this, the President of the United States Mr. Donald Trump is proposing a Space Force. I am in agreement with this idea. I feel that as countries like Russia have a joint Air and Space Force, the United States should also have a Space Force. We need a Middle Eastern NATO by the year 2030. In 2030, it will operate throughout the Middle East. By 2040, it should operate throughout the world in conjunction with the European NATO and with help and support from the United States. By 2050 and 2060, we should have a joint Middle Eastern Space Command, not necessarily a space force, but a space command, that will be staffed by members of all countries of the Middle East. This will be similar to how Europe has a European Space Agency. In this fashion, the Middle East will be considered a Global Leader, along with the U.S., the U.N., the EU, and NATO countries.

Chapter 19: Why This Would Be Good For U.S. National Security And U.S. Geostrategic Goals

A Two-State Solution, with an Israel and Palestine with clear, defined borders, clear, defined militaries, clear, defined economic cooperation, and clear, defined security cooperation, would be good for the United States. It would create a domino effect in terms of international peace movements. North and South Korea may reunite to form a united Korean Peninsula. India and Pakistan may make peace. And Israel and Iran may even one day achieve peace with each other.

Giving Palestine military technology from the United States would allow its leadership to keep the peace in their country. Giving Israel a slight qualitative and quantitative edge by giving it F-22s and Los Angeles Class Submarines would insure that even a smaller Israel would remain secure.

And finally, not only would our (the U.S.'s) oil supply become more secure with less volatility in the oil market, but we would be able to eventually withdraw all troops from Iraq and Afghanistan within the next five to ten years from when I am writing this (2018). We would then also be able to remove about, let's say, 25% to 30% of U.S. Troops from the Middle East and allow for those troops to be moved to places like Eastern Europe and East Asia, which are seeing a rise in the possibility of larger conflicts forming, as in the conflict between pro-Russian separatists and Ukraine and the North and South Korea conflict possibly becoming greater in scope.

Chapter 20: Me Personally

As I sit at home writing this, I feel that Middle East peace is possible. I know I am just a simple former Army Admin Clerk and Bachelor's Degree level University graduate. But having said this, I feel that the plans laid out in this book may very well work. If they are put in place and succeed, then my service in Kuwait may make me one of the last million or so Americans (Operation Iraqi Freedom and Operation Enduring Freedom Veterans) to have served in a major campaign in the Middle East. Many more will serve in the Middle East but not in as great of a number as in Iraqi Freedom and Enduring Freedom, I hope. In the future, if plans like mine are put in place, then the Middle East will be a more peaceful place and we could very well focus on other regions of the world, security-wise, like I said in the previous chapter about U.S. National Security interests.

Conclusion

With my military experience, my time spent in the Middle East, and with my Political Science studies, I have realized that governments can and do talk to each other. But now, it's time for the people to talk to each other. NGOs/Nonprofits should help everyday people, both in Israel and in the Palestinian territories, speak to each other. They should give everyday people a voice in the Peace Process, for it is the people that live through war and live through peace as well. I firmly believe that governments should talk to each other and the people should talk to each other. We all have differences and we, all of us, have at least one thing in common. The people should also talk to their governments to affect change, and governments should ask their people how they would like to see change as well.

A durable peace is necessary for both the Israelis and Palestinians. This conflict is not sustainable. I have to reiterate this again. This conflict is not sustainable. If the Middle East wants peace and to put themselves on a global stage, then they need to fight for peace. We need to see a Two-State Solution within the next ten or twenty years, that way, Israel and the Palestinians would be able to create joint partnerships, such as a Middle Eastern version of NATO, which could spread to include other Middle Eastern countries, and this would make the Middle East, to include Israel and Palestine, a global leader, along with the U.S. and other U.N. Security Council Members. But this will take time. I foresee something like this happening not today or tomorrow. But in one or two decades' time. The key, though, is that the work I have proposed has to start today. It has to start now. If we start now, we will have the Middle Eastern Space Command by the year 2050 or 2060.

This would be good for U.S. National Security interests because this would allow for the U.S. to transfer military and political resources to other parts of the world other than the Middle East. Parts of the world that are seeing a rise in tensions. I personally feel that peace in the Middle East would allow for us to have less future military involvement in the Middle East which would lead to more involvement in other, even more volatile regions of the World.

As a final note, I will reiterate again that we should remember that everyone has at least one thing that they all have in common with someone else, no matter how different we may seem. And I will always remember my time in Kuwait, Qatar, and Israel. That I will never forget for it gave me hope for peace in the region.

Thank you for reading this book. Take care now.

Introduction To Jerusalem 2100 AD

This book will serve as a follow-up to my previous book, *Kuwait, Qatar, And Israel*. It will discuss the Middle East from the year 2018 AD through 2100 AD. I will speak about why I support a Two-State Solution, why Israel and Palestine need security guarantees from the United States, the need for a Middle Eastern NATO, why peace would be good for U.S. strategic long term goals, and a Middle Eastern Space Command, among other ideas going into the future. I will even introduce what I call The Conservative To Liberal Approach To Governing A Country.

Chapter 1: Israel And Palestine In 2025 AD

2025 AD is the date I set as a deadline for the Israelis and Palestinians to achieve a just settlement and acquire a Two-State Solution and end their conflict permanently. Some may disagree with me and say that a One-State Solution is needed. The problem with a One-State Solution is the logistics. Israel and Palestine should be separate states and not one big state because it would be easier to manage a smaller and more secure Israel for the Israeli Government and it would be easier for the Palestinians to manage a smaller and more secure Palestine. As I am writing this (in 2018), Mahmoud Abbas is the President of the Palestinian Authority. Benjamin Netanyahu is the Prime Minister of Israel. Just based on these last two sentences, we already have a framework for peace. We already have a Palestinian Authority that can be put in charge of both Gaza and The West Bank in case a Palestinian State is established, which I feel it should be established by the year 2025 AD. We already have an Israeli cabinet with proper infrastructure that will continue to lead an already existing Israel when a Palestinian State is created.

To create a One-State Solution, we would need to combine the governing bodies of Israel and Palestine into one unit. We would then also have to combine the military and infrastructure spending of both countries into one unit. We would then have to draft an entirely new Peace Treaty and an entirely new agreement on borders. This will cost both the Israelis and Palestinians so much money. So you can see, this money can be used instead to help both of their peoples. This is why I support a Two-State Solution.

How would I formulate a Two-State Solution? I would have Gaza and The West Bank be part of the Palestinian State while Israel would have full control of Pre-1967 Israel. Israel already withdrew from the Gaza strip in 2005 and all that is really left is to withdraw from The West Bank. No withdrawal from East Jerusalem is necessary as whoever is in East Jerusalem, whether Jewish, Christian, Muslim, or Armenian, will stay in East Jerusalem. First and foremost, we need an Israeli withdrawal from The West Bank. The negotiations on East Jerusalem will come later. But I personally believe, like I stated in my last book, *Kuwait, Qatar, And Israel*, that East Jerusalem should become a capital of both Israel and

Palestine. I will expand on my previous idea that I put in my last book.

Israel and Palestine would share East Jerusalem. The Christian Quarter would be jointly shared and staffed by both Israel and Palestine, with Israeli and Palestinian Christians overseeing the Christian Holy Sites. Israel would oversee the Jewish Holy Sites like The Wailing Wall. Palestine would oversee the Muslim Holy Sites. I have to add one thing I did not mention in my previous book. Israel would have complete control of The Wailing Wall on the condition that Israeli Muslims and Christians and Palestinian Muslims and Christians would also be able to pray at the Wailing Wall the way Israeli Jews and Jews worldwide are able to do. Palestine would have complete control of what is known to Muslims as The Noble Sanctuary and known to Jews as The Temple Mount on the condition that Israeli Jews and Jews worldwide would be able to pray inside of it the way Muslims and Christians would be allowed to pray at the Wailing Wall. Like I stated in my previous book, the Armenian Quarter would continue to be staffed by Armenians and would be either part of Israel, Palestine, or both, depending on the Armenians' discretion.

Israelis would live in pre-1967 Israel and Palestinians would live in the State Of Palestine, in Gaza and The West Bank. Israeli settlers who wish to remain in The West Bank would be considered Israeli Citizens living abroad in The State Of Palestine. Palestinians who wish to live within the State Of Israel would be considered Palestinian Citizens living abroad in The State Of Israel.

East Jerusalem residents would either be Israeli or Palestinian Citizens, based on whether they are Israeli or Palestinian, which is basically self-explanatory. Palestinians who wish to travel from Gaza to the West Bank and vice versa would travel on normal Israeli bus and train routes but would be escorted by Israeli Police and Israeli Military for their own safety.

Chapter 2: The Conservative To Liberal Approach To Governing A Country

Just as Israel and Palestine would become separate states, we need all of the countries in the world, which are now numbered at 195, to be separate states. Why do we need this conservative approach of having countries and not having entire continents form states? The answer is limited resources. We need a country to have a President or Prime Minister that manages the already scarce financial and natural resources that that country has. That is why the United States is not yet part of a North American Union. Why Africa is not part of An African Union. Why The Middle East is not part of a Greater Middle East Union.

We probably only have enough oil and natural gas for about 100 years or so remaining. That is why it is crucial to have smaller country units, rather than continent level countries, to share these natural resources. That is my conservative approach to governing a country. With less resources and less people to govern, each of the 195 countries can continue to manage their people efficiently.

In the year 2060 or maybe it might come later in 2100, we would have what I call the liberal approach to governing a country. As I am writing this book (in 2018), Miguel Alcubierre Moya, a Mexican Theoretical Physicist, is working on formulating equations for the Alcubierre Drive. This Drive would propel spacecraft at faster than the speed of light speeds. The country of Iran has talked about building the world's first fusion reactor. The President of the United States, Mr. Donald Trump, has talked about creating a U.S. Space Force to be the Sixth Branch of the U.S. Military. The Space Force is to come to fruition in the year 2020 AD.

All of these technological innovations, such as faster than light speed, nuclear fusion, and the U.S. Space Force, will lead to us having more energy resources. Nuclear fusion would give us much more energy than we already have, if not near-unlimited energy. The Alcubierre Drive will let us travel faster in space and then mine asteroids and meteors, and send the mineral resources we harvest back to Earth. The Space Force will be another addition to the already existing NASA and other space organizations on Earth which will give us more drive and motivation to explore space. Then when we harvest near-unlimited energy, either in the 2060's AD or the 2100's AD, it will be easier for leaders to govern larger swaths of land more efficiently due to more resources being available for more people. We would then be able to have a North American Union consisting of Canada, The United States, and Mexico, an African Union, a Middle Eastern Union, a European Union which would include Russia, and an Asian Union.

Chapter 3: Security Guarantees For Israel And Palestine

By now, in this book, we are talking about the year 2025 AD, and Israel and Palestine have agreed to the Two-State Solution and are now living side by side as brothers and sisters in peace. We, The United States, need to ensure security guarantees for both sides. I will expand on my earlier comments from my book *Kuwait, Qatar, And Israel*. In that book, I mentioned giving Palestine several U.S. tanks, Humvees, and helicopters, and giving Israel two Los Angeles Class Submarines and ten F-22 fighter jets. By 2025 AD, I hypothesize that the U.S. would already have mostly stealth fighter jets even more advanced than the F-22 and its submarine fleet will be far more advanced than the existing Los Angeles Class Submarines. And its tanks, helicopters, and Humvees would be faster, stronger, more resistant to damage, and stealthier.

That is why I feel that it would not hurt U.S. National Security by giving Israel and Palestine double the technology that I proposed in my last book. For its own internal security, I would give The Palestinian Authority of Palestine ten M1A1 Abrams Tanks, thirty armored Humvees, and fifteen Apache helicopters, as well as many troop transport helicopters and armored troop transport carrier vehicles. I would give Israel five Los Angeles Class Submarines to replace their fleet of five diesel German-built submarines and I would give Israel twenty F-22 fighter jets. I would also give Israel twenty M1A1 Abrams Tanks.

The steps outlined in the previous paragraphs of this chapter would ensure both domestic security for Palestine and a slight quantitative and qualitative edge for Israel, thereby giving both countries a sense of internal security as well as external security for the Israelis. By the year 2030, the Israelis and Palestinians can form joint intelligence and security-sharing partnerships, which will lead the Middle East to have a greater security-sharing partnership like Europe's NATO. NATO has worked successfully to counteract The Soviet Union for many decades as well and that is why it is a good model for the Middle East to follow. NATO also functioned well in The War On Terrorism, and that is yet another reason for it to be used as a model for the Middle East.

Chapter 4: Israel And Palestine In 2030 AD

Israel and Palestine would increase security cooperation by 2030 AD. They would convince all armed non-government factions such as Hezbollah and Hamas to disarm as there is peace between Israel and Palestine and no need for further fighting. They would have a two country security cooperation which would lead to a greater security cooperation in all of North Africa, The Arabian Peninsula, Turkey, and Iran.

Initially, since relations in 2018 AD are improving between Israel and Saudi Arabia, I feel that Israel, Palestine, and the Arabian Peninsula states will form a joint security pact in 2030 AD. This Israeli-Palestinian-Arabian Peninsula Pact will then negotiate with Iran to not work on nuclear weapons capabilities, but instead to focus only on peaceful nuclear energy, such as the fusion reactor the Iranian leadership stated that it is working on. The UN, The U.S., and the Arabian Peninsula countries, and Israel and Palestine will oversee Iranian nuclear development and ensure that it is peaceful. Iran then will work together with this Israeli-Palestinian-Arabian Peninsula Pact to create peace in places like Yemen, which are seeing a rise in hostilities in 2018 AD.

Chapter 5: The Middle East On A Global Stage In 2040 AD

By the year 2040 AD, Israel and Palestine will form a joint security pact with not only the Arabian Peninsula, but with Iran, Turkey, and the North African States. Turkey will have the distinction of being the first NATO member to be part of both this Middle Eastern Alliance and NATO as well.

I feel that this will definitely give the Middle Eastern countries more standing on the World Stage. During the Cold War, most of the Middle Eastern countries were considered non-aligned nation-states. I feel that a Middle Eastern NATO would help bring about a change in world opinion. Middle Eastern countries that were once considered non-aligned will now be major decision makers, along with the U.S., The European Union, and Russia, among others.

In 2040 AD, China and Russia will become more powerful. They may very well become superpowers the way the United States is a superpower now in 2018 AD. There may very well be peaceful negotiations with Russia and China to form unions with them, such as finally brining Russia into NATO and bringing China into an Asian Union.

In one of the previous chapters, I spoke about liberal and conservative approaches to governing a country. By 2040 AD, we will be in an in-between period. We will have a period where countries will have better technology to harvest existing natural resources. This will allow for more continent-wide partnerships. Who knows, Russia may even join the European Union by 2040 AD. We will wait and see.

But just as the U.S. and other countries have given financial and military aid to the Middle East, I feel it is time for the Middle East to give back to the world at large. I feel that it is not enough for the Middle Eastern version of NATO to only patrol and secure Middle Eastern countries. By 2040 AD, the world will be even more global than it is today and the NASWAA (North African-Southwest Asian Alliance), which I will call it for the rest of the book, will go on security operations all over the world. NASWAA is the name I gave for the Middle Eastern version of NATO in my previous book, *Kuwait, Qatar, And Israel.*

Chapter 6: Eastern Europe And East Asia In 2040 AD

We, the United States, may not yet have a complete working relationship with Russia and China in 2040 AD. We may yet have some disagreements. By 2040 AD, Russia and China may become superpowers like the U.S. is currently a superpower. That is why NATO and the NASWAA may very well have to deploy to Eastern Europe and East Asia, for security reasons. In 2018 AD, there are battles in Eastern Ukraine between Pro-Russian separatists and the Ukrainian Government. In East Asia, in 2018 AD, there is still conflict between North and South Korea.

We should encourage Russia to convince the Pro-Russian separatists to lay down their arms, and we should encourage Russia to give back the Crimean Peninsula to Ukraine, and in exchange, Ukraine will work with The European Union, Russia, and the United States for a peaceful solution. And in the future, Ukraine may very well work with The European Union, Russia, and the United States, all on equal terms, to avoid conflict with any of the three. This is how we would avoid any future conflicts with Russia.

In East Asia, North and South Korea are still in conflict. I support Mr. Trump's steps in negotiating peace between the two countries of the Korean Peninsula. Also, China is becoming stronger, both financially and militarily. In order to avoid conflict with China in the year 2040 AD, I feel we need to support Mr. Trump's steps in negotiating for better trade deals. All of these steps I mentioned in this paragraph and the previous paragraph will help prevent future wars around the year 2040 AD and will lead to even a superpower Russia and superpower China to live peacefully with the superpower United States.

The NASWAA countries of course, along with NATO, in the near-term, around 2030 AD or so, will of course have to deploy to Eastern Europe and East Asia to help secure U.S. and NATO interests there. But by 2040

AD, hopefully there will be peace in Eastern Europe and East Asia.

Chapter 7: U.S. National Security Goals And The NASWAA In 2040 AD

By 2040 AD, the NASWAA is formed and is going on security missions all over the world. No longer are non-aligned nations of the Middle East non-aligned, but are global leaders on the world stage. I said in my previous book, *Kuwait, Qatar, And Israel*, that Israel and Kuwait only have a few skyscrapers in Tel Aviv and Kuwait City, respectively, and smaller concrete buildings everywhere else, but this will change in 2040 AD. In 2040 AD, there will be many Dubai-style hotels that are thousands of feet tall throughout the Middle East. There will be many monorails and anti-gravity trains, anti-gravity busses, and anti-gravity cars, as well as flying cars. For those of you that haven't read my previous book, *Kuwait, Qatar, And Israel,* I want to make a confession. I am scared of heights. In the future, buildings will mostly be thousands of feet tall and there will be flying cars. But in the future, we will probably have pills or therapies that cure the fear of heights. So by 2040 AD, I will probably have nothing to fear.

Peace in the Middle East would create, by 2025 AD and 2030 AD, a more stable and more secure oil supply, which will work for the U.S. in the short and intermediate term, until more near-unlimited forms of energy are created. Having a stable NASWAA that not only patrols its own borders in the Middle East, but patrols the whole world, with the help of NATO and the U.S., only strengthens both U.S. and Middle Eastern security positions. It strengthens U.S. positions in that it shows that we can partially exit the Middle East to deal with conflicts that are boiling elsewhere. It strengthens Middle East positions in that the Middle East will, in general, have a greater position on the world stage. By 2040 AD, The U.S. and the NASWAA will have an equal position on the world stage, along with China and Russia, and The European Union.

Chapter 8: The Middle Eastern Space Command In 2060 AD

Just like the United States has NASA, and Europe has a European Space Agency, the NASWAA should have its own Space Command. Headquartered in Tel Aviv, Algiers, and Baghdad, it will have three headquarters initially and will send astronauts into space. By 2060 AD, countries like Iran and Israel and Palestine will have some of the greatest space launching capabilities known to humanity.

By 2060 AD, the NASWAA, the UN, NATO, and the U.S., will have by now worked for many decades with Iran on peaceful nuclear energy development. By the same year, Iran and Israel, the U.S., India, China, and Russia would have developed some of the world's first nuclear fusion plants. These plants will provide near unlimited energy. This will allow the world to work on better shuttle and rocket programs for space travel.

Former adversaries, now friends, Israeli and Iranian scientists will go into space together. India and Pakistan, inspired by the Israeli-Palestinian Peace Process and success of it, will send astronauts into space together. A united Korean Peninsula will send astronauts to space together.

Chapter 9: A Conservative Approach To Nation-States Gives Way To A Liberal Approach To Nation-States in 2100 AD And Beyond

By 2100 AD, we will have the Space Forces of the world as not at the forefront of fighting wars on Earth, but of stopping threats from outside the planet like rogue asteroids. By 2100 AD, nuclear fusion will become the primary source of power for the planet. We will then have more energy for more people. Countries will soon become partnerships on a continental scale that will not fight but will compete with each other to see who can make the future even brighter first. The Middle East will have a partnership which will be called The Middle Eastern Union. Mexico, Canada, and The United States will have a North American Union. The already existing European Union will now include Ukraine and Russia, living together in peace. East Asia will have an East Asian Union to include China and a United Korea. Conservative approaches to countries will give way to liberal approaches to countries. We will now go down from 195 countries to seven continents. Each continent will have one President and one Congress, based on the Original U.S. Constitution, signed in 1776 AD.

By 2200 AD, we may very well have the Alcubierre Drive functioning and we may be able to go at faster than light speeds and harvest mineral resources from asteroids. Unlimited fusion power and mineral resources from asteroids will give us the ability to create a world government in 2300 AD. This Government may be called the United Nations still, and it will be given more power, or it may be something different altogether.

Chapter 10: Jerusalem In 2100 AD And Beyond

By now, in 2100 AD, most countries in the world have now formed closer economic and security partnerships and are now working at the continent level. Israel and Palestine, which started as a Two-State Solution, is now a One State Peninsula, and part of a Greater Middle East. Jerusalem will, as it always was, be a welcoming place for Jews, Christians, and Muslims.

But by now, we will have even more liberal interpretations of religion as space travel becomes more routine. And by 2200 AD and 2300 AD, we will have colonies on Mars as well as outside our solar system, by at least several light years away from Earth. By the way, a light year is 6 trillion miles and the Milky Way Galaxy is 100,000 light years across.

Conclusion

From a Two-State Solution to the Israeli-Palestinian conflict, to the entire world exploring space, this book covered the story of what I think will happen not just in the Middle East from 2018 AD through 2100 AD and beyond, but what will happen in the entire world through 2100 AD and beyond. We will have Middle East Peace, eventually followed by continental and then global partnerships. We will then set out to explore space where former adversaries will travel both inside and outside the solar system, now as brothers and sisters.

Introduction to Spaceship Palestine, Spacecraft Israel

It is the year 2167 AD. Faster than light speed has just been achieved. Religion is slowly losing its influence on the planet. A Two-State Solution to the Israeli-Palestinian conflict has been achieved by the 2030s AD. By 2100 AD, nuclear fusion has become ubiquitous as an energy source on Earth. We have so much energy that we can provide for all 16 billion people on Earth, 2 billion on Mars, and 500 million on the Moon. Now, in 2167 AD, we have 7 continents and no longer have the individual 195 countries. In 2060 AD, the world decided that with the birth of nuclear fusion energy, we can provide more resources for less money and for more people. As a result of the end of warfare here on Earth, since we moved away from natural resources and towards nuclear fusion, and therefore eliminated poverty, we have a state of peace.

In 2100 AD, the United Nations dissolved itself and the world felt that since the United States of America's system works best, we can have a group of seven Continents rather than 195 countries. They proclaimed that the U.S. Constitution was the best and worked the best, so every continent in the world now became a country. We have the North American Union, the European Union, The

Asian Union, The African Union, The Antarctic Union, The South American Union, and The Asian Pacific Union. They each have a Congress (House and Senate), Presidency, and Supreme Court. This is just like the three branches of Government in the United States. Israel and Palestine, being the last bastions of religion on Earth, became part of both the African Union and Asian Union, as they are part of a mini-union called The Greater Middle East.

Chapter 1: Daniel and Suleiman

It is sunrise in the greater Middle East. It is June 2167, about one hundred years after the Six Day War of 1967.

Daniel, an Israeli member of the Greater Middle East Military Command, based on the U.S. Military, approaches Suleiman, a Palestinian member of the Greater Middle East Command, and says, "Suleiman, hello." Suleiman replies, "Hello." Daniel says, "Can you believe it is 100 years after the Six Day War? How stupid were humans back then to fight each other?!" Suleiman responds, "It's just the way things were. We had limited land. We had limited resources. We had poverty. We had all these problems. Now things are better."

Daniel states, "Yeah, I guess. Now that we've had light speed space travel here on Earth for several years now, and we've met alien life and harvested asteroids for natural resources, and we have nuclear fusion, and plus the technology that the aliens gave us, we have a lot more now. But we need to do better. I need to do better. I still have never left Earth. My religious father does not want me to leave the planet because he said God created the Earth for humans and nothing else belongs to humans other than Earth."

Suleiman said, "Don't worry. You'll visit the moon, Mars, and other star systems soon enough."

Daniel states, "Yeah, I hope so."

As soon as they are finished talking, a loud engine noise emanated from behind them. The two of them turn around. A big old 2020's AD motorcycle, all black, approaches their desert post. When the motorcycle stops and is parked, a six foot tall figure in black leather boots, black leather pants, a black cotton tank top, and a black leather biker jacket with a white helmet on steps off. The figure slowly takes off the white helmet and reveals a blonde hair, blue-eyed woman's face. She puts the helmet on the motorcycle and slowly steps off the bike. The leather creaks loudly as she walks towards Daniel and Suleiman.

Daniel and Suleiman, in unison, state "Good morning, Doctor R."

Doctor R. replied, with a British accent, "Good morning." While only 37 years old, Doctor Jessica R. is one of the most renowned faster than light scientists in the world and earned her doctorate at age 27, one of the youngest PhDs that Daniel and Suleiman knew. She is also one of the top graduates at the European Union School of Theoretical Physics. "I'm late. Sorry about that. I better go into the lab. Come with me," stated Doctor R. Doctor R. went into the lab complex, a giant several hundred feet tall white dome. As she entered the building, followed by her guards, Daniel and Suleiman, she showed them the Jericho 10. While much of Israel has many buildings that are thousands of feet tall, being the year 2157, the Negev desert is still pretty much a desert. And this is probably the biggest object in the entire desert. The Jericho 10 is huge, it is a three thousand foot tall rocket.

"Ma'am, are you sure that we are allowed to be in here? This is the first time we entered the complex." Daniel asked.

"Yes, you are. You will be the pilots. This will be different. Every country in the world has achieved speed at 2.5 to 3.5 times the speed of light. This will be the first flight at 7, 8, 9, and maybe even 10 times the speed of light. Let's just say that we perfected Einstein's equations."

Suleiman gasped and then stated, shocked, "But we're just Middle Eastern Union military guards. We're not part of any space command!"

Doctor R. replied, "At ease, Soldier. We read your psych profiles and you are the perfect ones for this mission. You always put others before yourself and you care about the world around you. You are the perfect ambassadors for humanity."

"Is that a Jericho missile? Because that is what it says in Hebrew and Arabic," Daniel asked.

Doctor R. stated, "Yes, it is. It is the Jericho 10. It will.."

Daniel interrupted, "But I thought it was not in service after the world dismantled all nuclear weapons?"

Doctor R. said, "Yes. But we created the latest version to carry the Capsule, which will have the latest faster than light engine."

Chapter 2: The Capsule

The Capsule is the latest in space age technology. The Capsule is the most aerodynamic within Earth's atmosphere and the most efficient in space. The Jericho 10 rocket will help get it there.

Doctor R. told Daniel and Suleiman, "We are now at the age of one world. We are no longer going to have the seven continents anymore. We will have a one world government."

"It will be based on the U.S. Constitution, right?" Daniel asked.

Doctor R. said, "Nope."

Suleiman asked, "Will it allow the Middle East to keep our Jewish, Christian, and Muslim faith?"

Doctor R. said, "Nope." Then she motioned to the guards, "Guards, take them!"

A 6'5" large-framed guard wearing black leather combat boots, olive colored pants, an olive colored collar shirt, and a green helmet with black googles, hit both Suleiman and Daniel in the back of the head with a laser rifle. Suleiman was out cold. But Daniel began to recover, and as soon as he did, a laser weapon was fired at him by the tall guard. It did not kill him, as it was on a low setting, but it did stun him. When they woke up, they were inside a dome-shaped room.

"Uh, my head," Daniel said in between moaning in pain.

Suleiman recovered several minutes later. "Where are we?"

Doctor R. stated, "You are in the capsule. I am not Doctor R. I am her clone. I had to take her place at the behest of the One World Government. We are to take the last religious people and send them to an off-world penal colony. We cannot have God in a world like this."

Suleiman stated, "But Dr. R. once stated that the religious person and the atheist deserve equal respect. These were the teachings of 21st century author Vitaliy Balin."

The clone replied "Yes, but he was an idiot. How would he know what we are going through in the future? In fact, only a few of the alien races we have encountered embraced your so-called God and most of them do not embrace God."

Daniel yelled out, "Why does that matter!?" He wanted to fight off the guards that were next to him, but he could not as he was restrained on the chair in the capsule, as was Suleiman. When Daniel looked around, he saw there were hundreds of chairs in the capsule, and two of them had his father and mother there. "Aba! Ima!" He yelled in Hebrew. Those are his parents. "What did you do to my parents?!"

The clone angrily said, "You will not disrespect me! I merely sedated them! As far as you are concerned, I *am* Doctor R. and you will obey my orders. Your orders are for all religious people to go to an off-world penal colony and spend the remainder of your days there. The aliens will no longer respect us if we continue to have our primitive religions."

Daniel and Suleiman both exclaimed, "Primitive religions!? Religion is our life." The clone then sedated them. She and her guards then left the capsule and took a long elevator ride down to the main facility. Afterwards, they left the dome-like facility and activated the rocket.

The Jericho 10 rocket, that is 3,000 feet tall, was filled with hundreds of the most religious followers on Earth. At least liberal religious followers. Because in the future, due to space travel and contact with alien life from other worlds, people became less religious but some still kept at least a small faith in God. But the clone and her bosses would not tolerate faith in a belief in God.

By now, the clone and her guards were a mile and a half away, watching the rocket take off from their trucks and military vehicles. The computer of the rocket was synced to their radios. They heard the countdown. A female computer voice counted down, "Ten.. nine .. eight .. seven .. six.. five.. four.. three.. two.. one.. lift off." The rocket launched and after several minutes was going up the Earth's atmosphere and eventually made it through the atmosphere. The main body of the rocket came off and the capsule with its faster than light engine was all that was left. The capsule reached a speed of 7 times the speed of light, much faster than most faster than light engines on Earth, and this only angered most of the Earth's leaders as well as the aliens that were at peace with those leaders. But it made the clone and her bosses happy, and the aliens that were allied with the clone's bosses were happy.

The clone quipped, as the ship left Earth, in her mind, forever, "Just as your Six Day War took six days, religion will be destroyed on Earth in six days and finally aliens will respect humans that much more in that we outgrew our Bronze Age superstitions."

Chapter 3: Spaceship Palestine, Spacecraft Israel

Most of the world's religious people, mostly from the Middle East, are now on that capsule. After eight hours, the ship comes to a halt. The lights are now no longer dim and light up the ship like daylight. Most people begin to regain consciousness. Daniel and Suleiman wake up and look at each other. Suddenly, their restrains all come free. After several minutes of grogginess, Daniel finds his family on the capsule and Suleiman finds his family.

Daniel tells his father, "I am so sorry aba that this happened to you. There has been a coup on Earth. A group called the One World Government is slowly but surely trying to take over the planet and outlaw all religion."

Daniel's father, Ephraim, said, "You have to not only follow God, my son, you have to find the manuscript that will change the world."

"What manuscript?" Daniel asked. "The Manuscript of Inclusion," his father replied.

Suddenly they felt and heard a loud knock on the side of the capsule. Then a door opened. A ship was docked with the capsule. What looked like a group of 20 seven foot tall guards dressed in all black armor and black helmets walked into the capsule. Finally the last two people walked out of the ship and into the capsule. They were two women. One of them was a white lady in her thirties at 6'1" inches tall. She had dark brown hair, slightly past shoulder length, and hazel-colored eyes. She was wearing black leather boots, black wet-look PVC pants, a black wet-look PVC t-shirt and a black nylon puffy down jacket. The second person that walked out of the ship and into the capsule was a 6'3" inch tall black lady in her thirties with black hair at shoulder length, black leather boots, black wet-look PVC pants, a black wet-look

PVC t-shirt, and a black nylon puffy down jacket. They were dressed the same basically.

The two women told their guards to stand down. The guards stopped pointing their weapons at the 100's of passengers and then held their plasma rifles at the low ready. They made two ranks. One line on one side and one line on another side. The two PVC-clad women approached Daniel, Suleiman, and Ephraim. The black lady in PVC asked Ephraim, "Where is The Manuscript of Inclusion?"

Ephraim replied, "I don't know what you are talking about."

The black lady in PVC stated, "I apologize for our rudeness. We did not introduce ourselves. I am Kerra and this is Sarah," she said as she pointed at the white lady clad in black PVC.

"Now that you know our names," Kerra stated, "I have to ask you again one last time. Where is The Manuscript of Inclusion?"

Ephraim said, "I have no idea what you are talking about." Then he swallowed in fear.

Sarah stated, "Guard, give me your plasma rifle." One of the seven foot tall guards gave Sarah his plasma rifle. She adjusted some settings on it, which gave off beeping sounds, and the she pointed it at Ephraim and pulled the trigger, vaporizing him instantly.

"Abaaa!!!" yelled Daniel, as he started running towards the empty space that used to be his father.

Kerra then shouted, "Bring her out!" Then another two seven foot tall guards on the ship brought out a six foot tall blonde lady in black dress pants and a white collar shirt with black leather dress shoes. She looked emotionally distraught.

Kerra went on, saying, "This is Doctor Jessica R. One of the founders of the faster than light engine. We had to replace her on Earth due to the fact that she did not agree with limiting religion, culture, and science on Earth so that the aliens leave us alone. She felt that studying religion, culture, and exploring science and space more would lead to human progress and peace with alien life. But we, The One World Government, know that there is no way we humans can continue science, religion, and cultural progress when certain alien factions will invade us for it. And that is why Sarah and I not only allied ourselves with one of the alien factions, but decided to lead it. Show him." She then gestured to one of the seven foot tall guards and he took of his mask, revealing a somewhat evolved reptile appearance.

Sarah then said, "You see, Kerra and I want to not have any dealings with any aliens from now on because if humans continue to explore space, we will not only meet good aliens, but hostile ones as well."

Daniel stated, crying, "Why did you have to kill my father?"

Sarah replied, "We are sorry we had to do that. But we cannot allow any intransigence. You could not save your father but you can save Doctor Jessica R." She then slowly pulled down her down jacket and threw it off to the side. "Fight me in a Mixed Martial Arts match. I know that is one of the things you are good at. If you can beat me and Suleiman can beat Kerra, then we will let Doctor R. live and go free. If you cannot, then she dies."

Daniel, who is only 5'9" and only slightly muscular, was out-matched by the 6'1" tall Sarah, whom, while strikingly beautiful, is slightly muscular as well. The guards made a circular perimeter around Daniel and Sarah. Daniel made the first movie. He jabbed at Sarah, striking her in the face, which only caused a slight tinge of pain and made her giggle. She then grabbed Daniel by the right shoulder with her right arm and put her left arm on his right hip, and put her right leg behind his right leg, thereby tripping him. She then jumped on top of him and proceeded to punch him in the face. He grabs her right arm, then traps her left leg with his left leg and grabs the wrist of her right arm with his other arm, and rolls her around until he is on top of her. But after he reaches top position, she rolls around and gets him in armbar. He struggles to get out, but can't, and starts tapping out.

Sarah senses the tap, and yells out, "Beg me!"

"Pleeeaaase!" Daniel states, and then starts screaming from the pain.

Sarah lets go and leans over in the direction of Daniel, stating, "You see, you lost. And so did Doctor R."

She then stands up and motions to one of the guards and the guard presses a few buttons on his plasma rifle and then shoots Doctor R., vaporizing her the way Daniel's father Ephraim was vaporized.

Kerra then joins in on the conversation. "Dr. R. and Ephraim were the only ones that knew the location of The Manuscript of Inclusion. So we had to get rid of them. Enjoy your pleasure cruise now. What did Dr. R. call it? Oh, yes, Spaceship Palestine, Spacecraft Israel." Then Sarah retrieves her nylon down jacket and puts it back on and Kerra and Sarah both leave back into the ship, followed by the twenty guards. As soon as they leave, they close the hatch behind them and go into light speed, leaving the area by about several light years if not hundreds of light years.

Chapter 4: Arriving on the Penal Colony Planet

The capsule, Spaceship Palestine, Spacecraft Israel, then went back into warp. Daniel's mother comforted Daniel and Suleiman reunited with his family on the capsule. You see, not only were they the last religious people on Earth, they were also some of the best scientists, philosophers, and inventors. The One World Government, led by Sarah, Kerra, and an alien group, did not want them to be on Earth any longer because meeting aliens more and more would help human progress but may lead to eventual war with aliens. But the late Ephraim, and others like him, knew that continuing to meet aliens and make peace with them was the only way that the Earth would succeed.

After several hours, the ship made a full stop in space.

Suleiman said, "Where the hell are we?!"

Daniel said, "I don't know. But why do they want to hurt human progress to protect their own interests? I thought humans moved beyond that long time ago."

A large space pod docked with Spaceship Palestine, Spacecraft Israel, and then sent several human guards on board. The human guard leader, a man named Thomas, stated, "You are all prisoners of The One World Government and you will be taken for re-education and re-training on how to be better humans."

They were then taken on the pod and the pod landed on a planet. They were handcuffed and some were even shackled. The 100's of passengers were mostly form the Middle East, but some were from the Americas, from Europe, from Asia, and from other parts of the world. Daniel and Suleiman were taken to their own cell.

"Lights out," a guard yelled out over a loudspeaker. And the lights were turned off. It was pitch black in the cell.

Suleiman said, "I'm sorry I dragged us into this. I was the one that convinced you to volunteer to guard the faster than light engines in the Negev Desert."

Daniel replied, "It's not your fault. But we do have to find a way out of here."

"Did you say a way out of here?" a third man in the cell whispered. "I am Farooq. I can help you find a way out of here. But you have to find The Manuscript of Inclusion. You see, it was written by a man who lived in the 20th and 21st century named Vitaliy Balin. In it, he talks about the fact that the religious man and the atheist deserve equal respect. He talks about the need for moderate approaches in politics to bring people together. He talks about peace in the Middle East and peace throughout the world. These seem like archaic concepts to some people today, but let me assure you, they are still very relevant to today's world."

Daniel exclaimed, "Yes! I remember Dr. R. spoke about these things. She spoke about a man named Vitaliy Balin who spoke of world peace."

Suleiman interjected, "Why would anyone think that a single book will bring world peace?"

Farooq replied, "It won't. But ever since The One World Government faction in politics had all books written before 2050 AD banned, it made the world dismal and gloomy, not to mention intellectually repressed. I have something for you." Farooq then pointed at the wall and he stated, "I am too old. I cannot escape from here. In order to hide evidence of an insurrection among the prisoners, I will kill myself and make it look like you killed me to try to escape. But you must hurry and I can only slow down the guards so much."

Farooq took a plasma grenade that he smuggled into his cell and set it on a medium setting, blowing himself up and the wall of the cell with it. A guard on the other side of the wall became dazed, and Daniel and Suleiman used their Mixed Martial Arts skills to disarm him and take his plasma rifle. After the guard recovered, he went to check up on a dying Farooq, whose body was partially torn apart by the plasma grenade. Then another guard came upon the cell and an alarm was sounded.

Daniel shot and killed the other guard with the plasma rifle he and Suleiman acquired from the first guard. Then Suleiman took the other plasma rifle from the second guard and they began to shoot out the locks of every other cell. As more guards came in, the prisoners began to overpower the guards and take their plasma rifles. A prisoner who was at the penal colony for many years led them up a concrete staircase and then up into a maze of tunnels. The guards caught up to them of course, and killed about twenty of the prisoners, but about three hundred managed to escape, including 90 of the 100 prisoners that were on Spaceship Palestine, Spacecraft Israel.

Chapter 5: The Escape

Daniel and Suleiman took charge of the prisoners, as did Nikita, a 6'4" tall muscular 60 year old half-Ukrainian and half-Russian man that was the one that was on the prison planet for many years. He began to give every other person a plasma rifle. "We have not enough for everyone," he stated in broken English with a thick Russian accent. "Just like in ancient battle Stalingrad. Every other person take rifle. When someone with rifle die, you take his rifle."

Daniel soon reunited with his mother and the rest of his family. And so did Suleiman. They encountered several guards but easily either over-powered them or killed them, due to the prisoners having over 300 in their ranks, and the guards having maybe ten or twenty nearby. But another alarm was sounded. This time, a station-wide alarm.

"We must hurry!' Nikita yelled out. He led them to the capsule security pods. Nikita, Daniel, and Suleiman began to load the prisoners into the pods. Since these were created by humans and not the lizard-like aliens that Daniel and Suleiman saw before aboard Spaceship Palestine, Spacecraft Israel, they were able to quickly figure out how to operate them and then taught Nikita. Nikita then designated the pilot for each craft and then taught them how to fly them.

Each capsule security pod was equipped with two plasma cannons and two laser torpedo cannons. They had room for twenty people each. By now, after 20 prisoners were killed by the guards, there were 280 prisoners left. So 14 ships took off. The planetary laser system took out 2 ships and the other 12 ships began to fire on the planet and used up all of their torpedoes, disabling many of the planetary lasers. Then they came upon Spaceship Palestine, Spacecraft Israel, which was adrift in space. Daniel and Suleiman, remembering what the real Dr. R.

told them, managed to board all 12 of the capsule security pod ships onto Spaceship Palestine, Spacecraft Israel.

Suleiman informs Daniel, "Daniel! There are twenty capsule security pods coming our way. Do we have any defenses?"

Daniel replied, "We do! But our best defense is to just get away!"

After the prisoners were securely on board, and after Daniel and Suleiman made sure that they were all reunited with their families, they went to light speed at three times the speed of light and got away from the capsule security pods that were chasing them. Word of this got to the clone of Dr. Jessica R., who was now in a lab in Australia and was wearing black dress pants, a white collar shirt, and a white lab coat. Her human guards and the seven foot tall reptile-looking aliens that arrived with Sarah and Kerra, whom were also in Australia, commented that they just found out that Daniel and Suleiman escaped.

Sarah and Kerra, whom were now wearing white full-body dresses, approached the clone of Dr. R. and told her this news. Infuriated, the clone of Dr. R. called for them to be executed at the first sight of them. Sarah and Kerra agreed, and stated that they will do this with their own hands.

Chapter 6: The Manuscript of Inclusion

Daniel and Suleiman asked what Nikita knew of the Manuscript of Inclusion. He stated that it was somewhere in a sector of space in the Milky Way Galaxy where humans fled to keep their cultural prospective intact. They set course for this sector. They landed on an Earth-like planet, with similar climate, and told the people there their story. The people's leader, a tall human gentleman, who was originally from the United States, welcomed them. He is a 60 year old black gentleman, 6'2" tall, whose great grandparents served in an organization on Earth that investigated crimes that affected United States Citizens on a national level. He told them about The Manuscript of Inclusion and brought them directly to it.

"My name is Jonathan," the 6'2" tall 60 year old black gentleman said. "The Manuscript of Inclusion is a book written by Vitaliy Balin. It was written in 2018 AD. It was known as his political collection, but now it is known as The Manuscript of Inclusion. This is because he believed in a peaceful solution to the Israeli-Palestinian conflict and believed in a moderately centrist third party for the United States. He always believed that everyone had one thing in common with everyone else, no matter how different they may have seemed, and he believed in and valued everyone."

Daniel stated, "Jonathan, so this brown leather-bound book is the Manuscript?"

"Yes," Jonathan replied. "And Mr. Balin's book is not the only one. The One World Government banned all books written before 2050 AD. They thought that they could control people by getting rid of religion, and older interpretations of science and thought."

Daniel asked, "Why would they do this?"

Jonathan said, "They want to Earth to remain insular and without exploration, or at least one leading alien faction wants this. And Kerra, Sarah, and their leader want this."

Suleiman asked, "Who is their leader?"

Jonathan replied, "He is a reptile-like alien disguised through surgical means to look and act human. But DNA tests will not be fooled of course. His name is Hans. He is thought by most people to be born in Germany and now runs The European Union. He will soon be elected The One World Government leader with headquarters in Switzerland. We do not want this. We want the One World Government Headquarters to be in my former homeland, one that I have not seen in over twenty years. One in The United States of America. And a peaceful one, like the times of my great grandparents, where great leaders like Bill Clinton, George W. Bush, Barack Obama, and Donald Trump made fair and reasonable laws. Not this One World Government under Hans."

Daniel and Suleiman studied The Vitaliy Balin Political Collection, now known in 2167 AD as The Manuscript of Inclusion. They found that they agreed with it. Daniel told Jonathan, "What do we do now though? How do we stop this One World Government?"

Jonathan replied with, "It is not safe to go home to Earth for you. Hans, the clone of Dr. R., and Sarah and Kerra have given orders for humans and the reptile-like aliens to kill you as you are considered a threat to humanity. But we have a way of stopping this. We will send a signal to Earth of all the books banned after 2050 AD and will make sure that the people of Earth now know what is going on. We have DNA samples that one of our intelligence officers and several of his intelligence agents on Earth found that reveals the true nature of Hans.

Daniel, Suleiman, and Jonathan then went down into an underground heavily-guarded building. In the building, they are greeted by two human guards. They then hear metallic clanking. A dark figure in a pitch black tunnel approaches them. After he comes near the light, it is revealed to be a cyborg. Part human and part robotic.

The cyborg begins to speak, "Hello, I am Vitaliy Balin. The Humans living on this planet kept me alive for the day that we can all go back to Earth and realize the dream of meeting more and more alien life and for Humans to spread out into the Galaxy and eventually throughout the universe, and multiverse, and even beyond."

Daniel and Suleiman are shocked. Suleiman asks, "How is this possible? How can a Human live hundreds of years?"

Daniel asks, "Why have we not heard of things happening like this on Earth?"

Jonathan stated, "Because the One World Government and its alien leader Hans fear that Human expansion into more of the Universe will be a threat to his alien species. But we all know that this is not the case."

Vitaliy states, "We can all live in peace as a Galactic Brotherhood and Sisterhood and eventually as One Universe, Under God, Indivisible, With Liberty and Justice for All. Just like the American Pledge of Allegiance."

Daniel asks, "Do you believe in God, Vitaliy?"

Vitaliy replies, in a cybernetic voice, "I am secular. But like I said in my books in the past, the atheist and the religious person deserve equal respect."

Jonathan states, "Vitaliy, it is time. We must send the message and the sample to Earth." Jonathan sends thousands and thousands of old books to Earth via the message from the planet they were on to Earth. They then send evidence that Hans is an alien and the true nature of the clone of Jessica R. The people rise up and realize what is being done to their planet by Kerra, Sarah, Hans, and the clone of Jessica R.

Chapter 7: An Insurrection on Earth Narrowly Avoided

Jonathan sends a final message to Earth from the cyborg Vitaliy Balin. In the message, Vitaliy says, "All Humans and All Alien Life deserve equal respect. The Atheist and the Religious Person deserve equal respect. We must find one commonality that each of us has with the other person no matter how different we may seem. We must continue to explore space for it will one day save humanity to branch out into the stars."

Jonathan, Daniel, Suleiman, their families, Vitaliy, and hundreds and hundreds of other colonists on this planet board a convoy of large vessel guarded by smaller attack ships and head to Earth, at 5 times the speed of light. After thirty hours, they make it to Earth.

They then present the cyborg Vitaliy to Humanity. The cyborg Vitaliy pleads with the people to not form an insurrection against Hans, Kerra, Sarah, and the clone of Jessica R. but to have a peaceful transition of power, which of course occurs.

Hans is revealed to be an alien and returns to his home planet. Sarah and Kerra agree to never do what they did ever again. And the clone of Jessica R., through therapy, becomes more like her namesake Jessica R. and agrees to help Humanity as well as any alien species Humanity encounters and agrees to no longer side with any hostile aliens.

Vitaliy, Jonathan, Daniel, and Suleiman and their families spend the remainder of their lives on Earth.

Chapter 8: 100 Years Later

100 years later, in the year 2267 AD, Humans have now settled every corner of the Milky Way Galaxy. They no longer fight each other or any alien species but compete to see who can come up with the greatest invention or the best way to better themselves first. A One World Government, headquartered in Washington, DC now is the main Earth Government. Nuclear fusion power, faster than light speed, and mineral resources form asteroids now are used and no one goes hungry and no one is suffering any longer on Earth.

A gateway into other Galaxies is being studied. This gateway will allow spacecraft to travel at 1000's of times faster than the speed of light. Humans will now live to be about 200 to 300 years old. Some decide to upload their minds into computers or become cyborgs or robots and will live to be 500 to 1,000 years old.

Chapter 9: 2000 Years Later

It is now 4267 AD. Humans have mastered intergalactic travel and now live an average lifespan of 1,000 years. The entire universe is now within reach and pretty soon humans will travel within the multiverse.

Chapter 10: 10,000 Years Later

It is now 12,267 AD. Humans are all over the universe and even most of the multiverse. They encounter energy entities that live billions of years and eventually learn how to evolve themselves into energy entities. By now, the average flesh and blood human lives to be about 1,000 years old. The average cyborg or robot or human brain uploaded into a computer lives to be about 10,000 years old. And those that become energy entities live for billions of years.

Chapter 11: A Million Years into the Future

By now, most of the multiverse is populated by humans and now the average naturally born human lives to be 10,000 years old. Augmented trans-humans now live hundreds of thousands of years. Energy entities that started as humans live for as long as the multiverse lives. Maybe we will find the meaning of life. Maybe we will find the origin of the universe and multiverse. Maybe we may even find God. Who knows? But these are all questions that we should be asking ourselves every day.

Conclusion

From the wrong One World Government, to the right one, this book explored why we should not fear exploring space for it is in our genes to explore and find out more about the world around us. Thank you for reading this book. Take care now.

About The Author

Vitaliy Balin served in the U.S. Army, including a deployment to Kuwait. He has a Bachelor's Degree in Political Science and writes about history, politics, and science fiction in his books. He is especially passionate about issues that involve solving the Israeli-Palestinian conflict.